Walter William Mundy

Canton and the Bogue

The Narrative of an Eventful Six Months in China

Walter William Mundy

Canton and the Bogue
The Narrative of an Eventful Six Months in China

ISBN/EAN: 9783337166946

Printed in Europe, USA, Canada, Australia, Japan

Cover: Foto ©Andreas Hilbeck / pixelio.de

More available books at **www.hansebooks.com**

CHAP.		PAGE
I.	MARSEILLES TO SUEZ	1
II.	SUEZ—ADEN—GALLE	13
III.	SINGAPORE—SAIGON—HONG-KONG	25
IV.	A SHORT *RESUMÉ* OF CHINESE HISTORY	39
V.	SOME REMARKS ON QUESTIONS SUGGESTED BY OUR INTERCOURSE WITH CHINA	55
VI.	HONG-KONG	71
VII.	CANTON	89
VIII.	RESIDENCE IN CANTON	103
IX.	RELIGIOUS CEREMONIES	116
X.	SOMETHING ABOUT "TEA"	130
XI.	A CHINESE DINNER	146
XII.	NEIGHBOURHOOD OF CANTON	167
XIII.	THE *SPARK* OUTRAGE	180
XIV.	REVIEW OF PIRACY IN CHINA	197
XV.	SUGGESTIONS AS TO SUITABLE MEASURES FOR REPRESSING ACTS OF PIRACY	217
XVI.	THE TYPHOON OF 1874	233
XVII.	CONCLUSION	254

CHAPTER I.

MARSEILLES TO SUEZ.

The shortness of my stay in China may seem to make it presumptuous for me to attempt to relate to the public the little that I saw which may be new or interesting to them; but considering that on no point is there so much ignorance and misconception as on all things connected with the Chinese Empire, and that fewer books of real merit have appeared about it than upon any other question of equal importance, even what I have to say may prove, in its way, to be not without some interest, and my imperfect knowledge may be of some utility. The chief good I should anticipate from my own observations would be, that it would be setting an example to those in whom a longer residence in and acquaintance with the country, together with greater powers of discernment and description, would all combine to make them produce a book that should be at once interesting from the novelty of their facts, and instructive from the depth and penetration of their views and suggestions. This is of course far beyond my aspirations, and I shall be more than satisfied if I can with success play the humbler part of pointing out the way to those who could achieve a much more brilliant success.

I may be pardoned prefacing with these remarks, and will conclude them by expressing the hope that my readers will give me their kind consideration in my retrospect, which recalls to me many events that I need hardly say are of a very painful nature.

I left England on the 10th of March 1874, and arrived in due course at Marseilles, where I embarked in the French mail steamer *Tigre, en route* for China.

To any person who has never before undertaken a long journey by sea, and who is about to become for the first time a sojourner for weeks on the watery deep with all its dangers and hidden mysteries there must always be a feeling of excitement at the uncertainty of the future immediately before him, although it is sobered down by the solemnity of the enterprise. It seems as if we were leaving behind us, with the last view of our fatherland, some landmark that we do our very best to fix on our memory for ever so that whatever may betide us in the new life we are just about entering upon, we at least have all our old one so impressed upon us that it may serve to solace us in disappointment, or reanimate us to fresh exertions, in order to be restored to the home we leave behind in grief intolerable, if it were not lightened by the hope of a return after a career more successful than we could with justice expect to result from a continued residence in the old country. It is this hope that alone encourages Englishmen to depart abroad in pursuit of fortune, seeking for it under conditions less arduous than are entailed on those who remain in England; but also let it be not forgotten that it is to their efforts that England owes that empire on which the sun never sets. So my thoughts were with "auld lang syne," as the fortifications of Marseilles grew fainter in the distance, and my imagination changed them into the white cliffs I had a few days previously said good-bye to, as I believed, for many a long year. How man proposes to himself a future out of his own heart, and how illusory it ever is! I was young, however, and full of sanguine expectations. The prospect before me seemed to me to be without any drawback, and on the horizon of my worldly career there seemed to be no cloud whatever; so I soon with light-hearted gaiety settled down to make myself comfortable, and being a good sailor, had not to go through the painful ordeal of getting my sea legs.

The *Tigre*, although by no means one of the latest build, is in some degree remarkable for a length considerably in excess of her other proportions, and her tonnage is about 3,000 tons gross. I will not show my ignorance of nautical matters by attempting to give any express description of her, although a certain amount of gratitude must always be felt for the good ship that has performed in safety a journey of many thousand miles. As a passenger I was naturally concerned more with her internal arrangements than with her outward good points, and her cuisine and other accommodation left nothing to be desired. Of course, on starting on a long voyage like this, preparations are made for regular amusements, in order to make it agreeable and seem as short as possible. The English passengers, as a rule, compare the Messageries maritimes unfavourably with our Peninsular and Oriental in this respect. They say that the French officers neglect to organize theatricals and musical *soirées* to speed the journey, and that fewer steps are taken to make it a more pleasant affair. Although I cannot speak of the Peninsular and Oriental service from personal acquaintance, it is most probable that it is much gayer and not so quiet as it undoubtedly is on the French line. Still, the latter has some advantages, which I will try to enumerate. In the first place, in many ways the officers are specially obliging and attentive to English passengers; who, I regret to say, are, as a rule, somewhat deficient in reciprocating their kindnesses. They always made it a point of having some surprises in the shape of little dishes *à l'Anglaise*, and many of them who could not understand English on our setting out were sufficiently advanced in a short time to carry on an ordinary conversation, so eager to learn, and so little ashamed to speak a strange language imperfectly were they. What a contrast to ourselves, who dislike to show our imperfections in any way, especially in conversing in a strange tongue.

Among the passengers were a good many Dutch, French, and some German; the French leaving at Aden for the Mauritius, and the Dutch at Singapore for Java and Sumatra. I was greatly struck with the courtesy and general information of the latter, who were very amusing and intelligent companions. They were full of praises of everything English, and some were well read in our literature. I may here also say that if their views of our colonial empire may be taken as a specimen of the general opinion among them, there is little to be feared from their jealousy of us, even in the Straits of Malacca. On this subject I will venture, however, to make some remarks further on; of course I have been speaking of the European, not of the Colonial Dutchman.

By the Messageries it is comparatively an easy thing to get a cabin for oneself, and more than two are seldom, if ever, put into one. The French diet, to my mind, is also more suitable to the limited exercise possible on board ship than our own more substantial mode of living.

The weather was everything that could be desired as far as Naples, where, however, having the misfortune to meet with a slight accident, I was unable to land; but I had a good view of that unrivalled bay. Our stoppage was not for long, however, and that night we passed through the Straits of Messina, and in the morning Etna was but a speck far in our rear. Nothing had occurred to remind me of my close proximity to Scylla and Charybdis. So far the weather, though slightly cold, had been fine, but it now changed suddenly, and became sufficiently rough to close the ports. We also had to pass through a thick mist, which obliged us to slacken to half speed, and made frequent soundings necessary. This mist was caused by the wind blowing clouds of sand from the deserts of Africa. Through these causes we were somewhat late in arriving at Port Said. We immediately went on shore, but as it was dark we saw very little of the town. We went to the Casino, which I thought—even after several days at sea, when any change is a relief—very stupid; and then to the Alcazar, where the performance, which exclusively consisted of women playing on violins and other stringed instruments, was well worth seeing. Even critically observed, the playing was good.

Few of us had much sleep that night, as the noise from coaling the ship was terrific. We commenced our passage through the canal early in the morning. Without giving any description of this wonderful piece of engineering, I may mention that as the main channel is only sufficiently wide to admit of one ship going through at a time, there are stations where ships wait until it comes to their turn, and the way is clear. The communication is kept up, and the traffic is regulated by telegraph. As far as feasible, everything makes way for the mail steamers. The best comparison to make to illustrate the mode of working is to the arrangements on a single line of railway. The simile is almost exact. We were stopped some time at Ismailia, where both the Khedive and M. de Lesseps have handsome palaces, to let some vessels pass. Here I saw the *mirage*, and it was with some difficulty I could persuade myself that the sight was deceitful. I felt grateful, however, that the illusion brought no punishment to me, and

I shuddered to think how awful the disappointment must be to discover the fallacy when one's life was at stake in the desert. The canal regulations oblige all ships to anchor at night; so when the captain will give permission, many go ashore to shoot jackals, or to visit the *café chantant* which some of the villages possess. I was not much prepossessed with the inhabitants of these villages, chiefly employés of the company; a greater set of cut-throat looking vagabonds I never saw.

Just before reaching Suez we were stopped to let the transport *Crocodile*, returning with troops from India, pass.

The Messageries steamers anchor in a bay two or three miles from Suez, so I did not see the town, but the neighbourhood looked very pretty and nice.

CHAPTER II.

SUEZ—ADEN—GALLE.

The next morning we left Suez, steaming through the Straits of Jubal, and saw in the distance the peaks of St. Catherine, the supposed Mount Sinai. The weather was remarkably fine, and the heat soon became—some days later than usual, though —so oppressive that a change to thinner clothing had to be adopted. The "punkah" or "fan" had also to be kept in motion. Two days after leaving Suez we were hailed by a native (Arabian) ship signalling for a doctor. We launched our boat, sending to them ours, who did not seem to like the project at all. For some reason or other there was some excitement on board,—some even talking of pirates, which had a visible effect on the courage of the poor doctor. The idea of a small boat attacking a large steamer was too ridiculous for the impression to last long. How it ever arose would be difficult to imagine. On reaching her they found it was a hoax. The owners, having lost their way, wanted to know whereabouts they were. They signalled for a doctor, as they knew that is the only one for which a mail steamer will stop. This vessel was a very pretty sight, being perfectly white, even to the masts. Altogether this stoppage delayed us some hours. We passed through the Straits of Bab-el-Mandeb, close to our strong island of Perim. This island presents a most repelling appearance, being nothing but a barren flat without a trace of vegetation,—the friendly light-house being the only thing for which a human being has to be thankful. This station for the military is a sort of penal settlement, and the guard has to be changed at frequent intervals by reliefs from Aden. Outdoor amusement is an impossibility in this uninviting oven.

We arrived at Aden some hours later in the night, landing the next morning, when we drove to see the sight of the town, viz., the Tanks, which are some distance inland, close to the English cantonments. These cavities are supposed to have existed as far back as four thousand years ago. When we took and fortified Aden we constructed reservoirs in them, which, as it often does not rain here for three, sometimes not for ten, years, are most useful in collecting the water during the wet seasons. We also connected these tanks; one now leading into the other with steps down them, and planted terraces round the sides of the rocks with acacia and other trees, which form a great relief to the eye, as nothing else green can be seen in the neighbourhood, the whole district being volcanic: indeed the town of Aden is supposed to be built in the crater of a volcano, and the bold precipitous rocks by which it is surrounded represent the sides.

We drove about in the native carriage, which is the same at Galle and Singapore, and is also called "Gharry" at each of these places. Strange to say, this inhospitable-looking place is rather liked as a station by the officers. The reason I believe is, that it is possible for them to save on their pay. There is no question at all, however, about their hospitality, all being most willing to give everyone a hearty welcome. It was very amusing to see the little blackies paddling about in the harbour in tiny canoes, from which, or even from the yards of our vessel, they would dive into the water for money, and we could see them distinctly fighting underneath among themselves to get the prize. They would also dive under one side of the ship and come up at the other, chattering all the while like monkeys. I was not sorry, however, to leave this place and get on, for by this time the end of the journey was every day becoming a matter to be looked forward to with greater pleasure.

On passing Cape Guardafui and the island of Socotra, we encountered a great swell, which made us roll very much,—the curious thing being that the sea to all appearance was perfectly calm; but I believe there was nothing unusual in this. The contrast to the heavy rollers of the Atlantic was very great to all appearance, but the effect on the steadiness of our vessel was certainly not less. From Aden to Galle—by far the most tedious part of the voyage—it takes seven to nine days, according to the monsoon. The weather was so sultry and oppressive that it was often impossible to stay between decks, and several nights I slept on deck in an arm-chair. We saw lots of flying-fish and shoals of porpoises. If the days could be complained of on account of the force of the sun, the nights were the more enjoyable, for the splendour of the moon and the evening breezes compensated to some extent for the extra heat of the day.

We arrived at Galle after nine days' steaming. The change of scene was extraordinary. I may say, it was not since leaving Naples that I had seen anything green. A fortnight's roasting in the Red Sea and Indian Ocean would be enough to make one greet with pleasure the slightest shade; but here we had immense woods coming down to the verge of the water, which made me long for their refreshing shelter. I hope I shall not be accused of exaggeration in saying that Galle struck me as the prettiest place, externally, I came across. If anyone doubts it, they had better make the experiment; and if they —as they must from England—go the same route as I did, I feel certain that their opinion, after the same culinary preparation, will agree with mine. But as to reach the gardens of the Hesperides many obstacles had to be overcome, so there are dangers to be encountered by those desirous of landing here.

In the first place, even to enter the harbour is no easy matter, and requires the most careful steering. As a warning, should we not keep true in the centre of the passage, there rises above the waves, only a few yards from us, the hull and masts of the *Arracan*, wrecked here some months before. Even when we have passed through this dangerous strait we have only accomplished half our task. There is so great a swell that we are obliged to land in boats, and to get into these boats is very awkward and difficult. It requires the greatest skill in choosing your opportunity, which must be immediately acted upon, or you will not escape without a ducking at the very least. Perhaps I speak with some of the bitterness of unsuccess, as I was among the unfortunate,—escaping however, luckily, with only half the penalty. All this inconvenience detracts something from the praise of Galle, especially as many ships are periodically lost here. Besides, there is so obvious and simple a remedy. Colombo, which is very little out of the direct line, and is a very thriving and large town, has a commodious and fine harbour, which is easy of entrance, and safe at all seasons. It certainly is slightly out of the route, but the advantages that would arise from making it the port of call far counterbalance the slight delay that might be occasioned by the change. But, somehow, all the world over, it takes a very long time to effect any improvement on what is. As far as my experience goes, I can endorse the saying of an eminent man—that we are not Conservative, but Chinese. It may be some consolation to think that all the world's the same.

We went to the hotel on landing, which is a capital one. The proprietor fed us remarkably well, and I tasted here one of the greatest dainties imaginable. I unfortunately did not get the receipt, but I can state the chief ingredients: curried prawns, flavoured with cocoa-nut milk and dry champagne. It was capital. We took gharries, drawn by very fine little ponies, and drove up into the country, over excellent roads. The scenery was very pretty, splendid trees overhanging the roads, and forming a perfect archway. Through the vistas of the wood we could see native huts —to all appearance clean and comfortable —and now and then a small temple, with the native gods. These were chiefly remarkable for the tasty manner in which they were decorated with flowers. We drove also to see the cinnamon gardens, which were some miles inland. The only drawback that I could see was the quantity of beggars who, as everywhere else in the East, pestered us for alms. We drove back to our hotel, where a crowd of Parsee merchants had assembled to receive us, exhibiting their wares, and demanding fancy and most exorbitant prices for everything. We were taken by a back way to see their shops and all their treasures. They offered us sapphires, rubies, pearls, etc.; but though we were fully awake to their tricks, we found it difficult to resist their cajoling arts when we had put ourselves into their den. For a ring for which they demanded £50, they accepted £5. Of course the majority of these fellows are arrant swindlers, palming off pieces of glass or bad stones on the unwary as gems of priceless value. Their whole system is supported by unlimited credit, they reckoning on catching you on your return. They are a fearful nuisance, but it rests with travellers themselves to put them down by discouraging them. But as a few great bargains are sometimes made, everyone tries to do the same, and the result is that these fellows thrive and make fortunes, as elsewhere, on the credulity of mankind.

Our stay here seemed to me too short. It was only for twenty-four hours; I could gladly have enjoyed another stay of equal length. That evening there was a tremendous storm, the lightning being most vivid. This I may call our half way house, it being also in distance only a little more than half done towards getting to the end of the journey. I now had the pleasure of being able to look back on so much successfully accomplished to sustain me in the latter half of this lengthy undertaking. I left Galle much refreshed by its pleasant scenery, although there we lost some of our fellow passengers, who were much missed and regretted.

CHAPTER III.

SINGAPORE—SAIGON—HONG-KONG.

Four days after leaving Galle, we were passing the north part of Sumatra, although at too great a distance to get a very clear view of Atchin.. Our course here lay through narrow straits between little islands; and, more or less, this is the description of the whole of the view of the strait down to Singapore.

These islands present the most beautiful appearance. They are absolutely covered with trees, which run down to the water's edge. I saw a very splendid sunset the evening we were passing through. The sun, sinking behind the tree-crested mountains of the islands, lit up the open sea with a glow of gold, or was reflected back from the woods and rocks of various islets; while that part of the sea nearest to the shore, being in close shade, was consequently perfectly dark. The contrast was most singular and striking. We arrived at Singapore without noticing anything particular, for, as I said, one description is sufficient for the whole of this route. The entrance to the new and small harbour, although extremely narrow, is most pretty, as it is fringed on either side with thickly-wooded islands; although here is added to the scenery some comfortable-looking and picturesquely-situated villas, and the smoke rising from behind the trees cheers the heart with its sign of hospitality. We again took gharries and drove to the town of Singapore, which is about three miles from the quay; and having lunched on our arrival, we started to see the Botanical Gardens, which are about four miles inland. The drive through the jungle the whole way was remarkably pretty, and the Gardens, even after this preliminary preparation, did not fall short of my expectations. We dined with a friend still further up the country, where I saw a most perfect punkah; it had five fans, instead of only one. We also saw the Governor's house, but at that time without a Governor. Sir Andrew Clarke had not then commenced his administration, although on my return his success, aided by the well-known graciousness and kindness of Lady Clarke, was the talk of the place. Everyone out there will join, while deeply regretting his short stay, in wishing him every prosperity in his new appointment.

At Singapore the diving boys were equally numerous and amusing, and there they showed remarkable quickness in discerning the English from the French passengers. To the former they would say, "Have a dive?"—to the latter, "À la mer." Here we lost our agreeable fellow-passengers the Dutch, who change for Java. I regretted much to part from them, as they had been especially kind to me. One of them, who had been ruined in Holland by giving security for a friend, was going out with his wife to Batavia, to try and make another fortune. We all heartily wished him every success.

As the Straits Settlement seemed but a short time ago to have assumed a certain importance as the subject of a political question, it may not be out of place to make here a few remarks on that point. The Dutch, as is well known, were once our most formidable rivals on the sea. Even when Blake, Sandwich, and Rodney had in successive generations fully proved our supremacy on that element, Holland still possessed many colonies, some of which now belong to us, and might, without untruth, claim to be our equal in foreign possessions. These she owed to the energy and genius of her own sailors, who for some time and at a certain period were unrivalled. Of all that imperial sway, Java and Sumatra are the two most precious relics.

It is no exaggeration to call these islands, in richness of soil and quantity and variety of products, the pearls of the East Indies. Mismanaged, as they are acknowledged to be, not a tenth properly cultivated, still they furnish the home country with a net profit in the shape of revenue of several millions. The Dutch in that part of the world acknowledge their shortcomings, and look with envy on what they consider the admirable manner in which our Indian settlements are managed. They are only too desirous to make the best of their promising territory; but, whether owing to real want of energy, or to being hampered by the home Government, little progress is made. Opposed to the long sea-board of Sumatra lie our settlements on the peninsula of Malay, with the great emporium Singapore at its extreme end. They are thus brought face to face with us; and in the necessary course of things, a time must come when we shall be obliged to take cognizance of their doings. There is no doubt but that the Dutch are aware of our gradual absorption of everything worth possessing in this direction.

They also see more clearly than we do ourselves, that Australia—that continent of the future—is bound to draw nearer to our Indian Empire. They see that one of these days they must meet. They feel themselves unable, for several reasons, to oppose any permanent resistance to the progress of these movements.

While possessing much of the ability and courage of their forefathers, they have perhaps allowed a prosperous life in rich colonies to render them more sluggish and less likely to seize any favourable opportunity. Their army is also chiefly composed of natives or of mercenaries of every country, and not to be trusted when brought face to face with regular troops. Even the pluck of the Atchinese was sufficient to baffle for long the numbers brought against them.

The Dutch feel the reality of all this; and the result is an intense jealousy, which shows itself by hampering us in all our intercourse with these islands. It would be an instructive lesson to anyone to work up how it was that, when we were foremost amongst the advocates of conquest and extension of dominion, we permitted these treasures to escape our grasp. Their position, their wealth, every reason of policy, both on its broad principle and on its narrower one of self-interest, demanded their occupation. Why did we give up our hold on Sumatra in Bencoolen in exchange for Malacca? Of course, this gives no right to take them now, even if that were feasible; and if Holland were to manage them properly there might never be any necessity. But the world is not large enough nor rich enough to permit anyone to mismanage that which is meant for the good of all. And eventually, if we neglect to interest ourselves in the question, if we are so purblind as not to keep a watchful eye on this quarter, we may find that some other power, for reasons certainly not of friendship to ourselves, will secure these prizes, and we with our eyes closed the whole time. It ought to be sufficient to point out that, as far as race goes, Holland is as much German as Alsace or Holstein; and even the independent Dutch might not object so much as is imagined to merge themselves in such a formidable power as Germany would then become by their alliance. Germany is fast creating a navy. She would, then, have harbours and colonies. Those of her subjects who shirk the military obligations by leaving the Fatherland would, perhaps the State might consider, be sufficiently usefully employed in establishing new or strengthening old colonies to allow them to be excused from some of the legal penalties they incur under present circumstances.

On leaving Singapore, and turning our prow northwards, I may say we were setting out on our last stage, although, by the

French packet, the journey is broken by a stoppage at their settlements in Cochin China. In three days we reached Point St. James, which is at the mouth of the Cambodia or Gamboge river. The contract of the Company with the French Government compels them to go up the river to Saigon, which is about sixty miles, and entails a tedious journey of about twenty-four hours each way; they are also obliged to make a stoppage there of twenty-four hours; so that altogether this arbitrary and really useless arrangement delays the arrival in China by three days. The river is very wide, but so shallow that it is only possible for ships to go up to Saigon when the tide is favourable. The banks are very low, so I could see the jungle extending for miles inland. The heat here was something fearful, and the farther we went from the sea the worse it became.

As the French are held to attach much importance to this settlement, it is perhaps some set-off against the delay to get even a slight glimpse of how they manage their colonies. Coming from Singapore to Saigon seems like a return to Europe. With its straight streets lined with trees, with its *cafés* retreating under the shade, and its boulevards of handsome shops, it seems almost exactly like a town of *la belle France*. Scarlet trousered officers, bronzed by an eastern sun to almost blackness, lounge about; and the political talk is no less lively than it is on a Parisian boulevard. Their system of ruling their colony is exactly similar to that in force in Algeria, and is purely military. The whole of the country is dotted over with small stations, and the natives are subject and must conform to the French laws alone.

This is somewhat different and opposed

to the course we have adopted in the management of our immense possessions in India. There we see the military entirely subsidiary to the civil authority. The Commissioner is the highest power. We openly acknowledge we only hold our authority in trust for the benefit of the natives, and we encourage them to show themselves capable of assisting us in governing themselves. This is far removed from the military system, pure and simple, followed by the French; and I do not think its advantages can be questioned.

There is a *Jardin des Plantes* and a public park about a mile from the town. There is a very good show at the former, especially some magnificent tigers. Close to this is the Governor's palace, which is reputed to have cost seven million francs, or £280,000. Altogether, Saigon would repay a longer visit, and the heavy jungles throughout the interior afford a splendid field for sport. Besides, it has great advantages as a starting place for explorations inland, and the opening up of the Cambodia would confer more advantages on the human race than the clearing out of the Oxus. The latter will open up a passage to the rugged steppes of Khoordistan and the Hindoo Koosh, but the former will open up the rich treasures of Siam and Burmah.

We sailed down the river again, and four days after leaving Point St. James we reached Hong-Kong. It was a very pretty sight to see the merchants' gigs, manned by Chinamen in different coloured costumes, coming off to welcome old friends from their own common home, or new ones who were coming out to be cheered by their hospitality.

My journey was over. Ten thousand miles, mostly by sea, is, under every circumstance, both of comfort and of fine weather, but a disagreeable and tedious task. Its end can be only greeted with relief. But when it is accomplished, although feelings of expectation have been for weeks uppermost in our mind, we go back and dwell on all the episodes and dangers of the journey; and we then, if but for a few moments, feel some of the debt we owe to that Almighty Providence that has carried us with safety to our journey's end.

There is also grief and a feeling of loneliness to think how many a mile lies between us and our home, where is all we love. Only the warmest welcome, only the truest friendship, only the greatest hope can make us bear up successfully. These in my case were all powerfully present, and soon I was reconciled to my new surroundings.

CHAPTER IV.

A SHORT *RESUME* OF CHINESE HISTORY.

Before commencing my narrative of residence in China, I will devote two chapters to preparatory matter, which will perhaps serve to give greater interest and consistency to what follows. In this chapter I will endeavour to give some slight sketch of the course of China's history, while in the next I will make some remarks that may seem naturally suggested by our connexion with the country.

The native accounts date their empire from a most remote period, but we have as yet no reliable record of the events which occurred in the infancy of this extraordinary people; and considering that the authentic history was destroyed by a sovereign (Chi-Noam-to, 200 B.C.) whose acts the learned disapproved of, because it was turned against him to establish precedents to prove his own bad government, it is highly probable that it will for ever remain shrouded in mystery. We know that the Romans received ambassadors from a country called Cathay, situated far to the east of the Indus; and we may not be wrong in accepting these emissaries as coming from that country which is the subject of this book. We are also aware that some Christian sceptics are reported to have retired thither in the first centuries of the Church; and I believe attempts have of late years been made to trace their descendants.

Fo-Hi, one of the first emperors, and the reputed founder of the empire, lived about

2000 B.C., and is supposed to be the same as Noah; but the first reliable historical personage we know of, is Confucius, who was born about 550 B.C. He is to the Chinese what Moses is to the Jews, and Mahomet to the Arabs. He is at once their lawgiver and their prophet, their example of morality and the highest and grandest type of their race. The descendants of this distinguished philosopher form the only hereditary nobility among the Chinese. During the first centuries the imperial rule was exercised by the family of Hong, but the rulers for several generations having fallen into all the vices of impotency, were, after a period of anarchy and confusion, succeeded by the Tang family, which had as its founder the great Taitsong. Their dynasty falling into the same state of effeminacy as their predecessors', gave place to new rulers; and this result was repeated several times, until the great Mongol conqueror Genghis Khan overran a great part of the kingdom, and his grandson Kublai Khan completed the task of conquest by subduing the whole country, and he and several of his descendants ruled from Kamschatka to Cochin. But the old epidemic soon seized the Mongol emperors as it had previously the Chinese. Inactivity soon take the place of energy, and the pleasures of debauchery succeeded the actions of ambition in the court of Pekin. The conquered inhabitants, from being accustomed to sneer at the degeneracy of their conquerors, soon resorted to measures to restore themselves to freedom and to regain the empire they once possessed. The revolt was successful, and their victorious general established himself at Pekin. He became the founder of the famous dynasty of Ming; and, not content with having expelled a conqueror, led victorious armies through Thibet and Tartary. The Ming period is the most popular among the Chinese, as the time of their chief greatness; and it would be unwise to leave out of consideration the fact that they recur to the events of that time with extreme fondness, for as changes of rulers have in no other kingdom been of more frequent occurrence, so it is not impossible that one more revolution may be added, and it cannot be confidently asserted that it will meet with no success.

The defeated Mongols sought refuge among the Tartars on the extreme north-western frontier of the empire, and several centuries later their descendants appeared once more upon the scene under the name of Mantchoos. For even the sovereigns of the house of Ming were not to be exempt for any great length of time from the faults of their predecessors; and when the state was divided into rival factions, in an evil hour the aid of the Mantchoos was invoked. Victory declared for the side they fought on, and as Hengist and Horsa in our history from victorious allies made the easy change to conquerors, so in China these fierce and irresistible Tartars seized the empire, and converted their benefactors and friends into their dependents. The first emperor of the new race, Chun-tchi, showed himself a sagacious and tolerant prince by honouring the prejudices of his new subjects and by satisfying himself with the real attributes of power without demanding any of its useless appendages.

The Tartar conquest was consummated in the year 1644, and Chun-tchi was succeeded in 1661 by his son Kang-hi, who in a long reign of sixty years proved himself to be the most enlightened prince who ever occupied the throne. His measures consolidated the power of his family, and it is mainly to him that it is due that the state of the country has been tolerably settled ever since. He at first had friendly inclinations for foreigners, and it was in his reign that the Jesuits first effected a permanent settlement. He made use of their knowledge to assist him in compiling a history, and also employed them on many works of national importance, notably the improvement of the calendar and the education of the masses. It was at this time that so many works were issued on China, and had the place of the Jesuit observers been as worthily filled of late years by the English merchants, there should be a much greater knowledge of the people and of their customs than unfortunately there is. Towards the end of Kang-hi's reign, however, the Jesuits fell into disrepute, and they were banished the court. Perhaps some of their theories as to the spiritual supremacy of the Pope were a little too freely uttered to please the spiritual father of a distinct religion. Whatever the reason, the fact remains the same, that Jesuit influence was at its height in his reign, and that, although still, scattered over the country, where perhaps no other white man dare venture, may be found representatives of this powerful society, it has ever since been on the wane.

Since this reign the internal history of China has been quiet. The Mantchoos are still the ruling caste. The dynasty of Tatsing still sways the sceptre. To all appearance the native Chinaman is contented, and the Tartar lords it throughout the land. The even tenor of their rule has indeed received one shock. I allude to the Taeping rebellion; and the result of that insurrection remained undecided until an Englishman solved the difficulty by leading an army from victory to victory; and Gordon and the Ever Victorious Army became the heroes of the day. The vanity of the victors, hurt by having to own their success as chiefly attributable to a foreigner, has received some salve in the successful destruction of the Panthays, who had of late years formed an independent power in the south-west; and military officialism has become more arrogant than before, on account of these recent laurels. The Taepings were indeed crushed; but the impressions of foreign residents are conflicting as to whether the Chinese are really well affected to the Mandarins.

Ta-whang-li, or Mighty Emperor, is the style of the potentate at Pekin, and his power is as unlimited as the most extended view of paternal authority sanctions. He is temporal and spiritual chief; and his person is considered so sacred that it is only recently that audience has been permitted to the representatives of foreign powers; and now it is done in such a manner as in any other country would be considered more insult than honour.

The Government is carried on by a council of four; but at the present moment it is vested in a Regency, and the Empress, mother of the previous sovereign, is the instigator of policy. The great Viceroys exercise a vast amount of influence, and in their respective provinces are supreme, particularly the ruler of the province of Chihli, by name Li Hung Chang, or the great Li as he is more usually called; who to great power and wealth adds all the energy and ambition of his ancestors. In theory, however, the Tu-che-yiven, or censors, have the right to superintend all things, and have a station independent of the Ministry. They fill a somewhat similar position in name to that the Ephors did in fact at Sparta; but they are entirely without the power of that formidable magistracy. They have some privileges, and may enjoy the doubtful pleasure of listening to measures being resolved upon by the boards of administration without having any option between silence and a futile opposition.

It is sufficiently evident even from these few facts that if the sovereign be not of an active disposition, and does not really act the king, there is plenty of field for ambition; and that backstair influence is much called into use to decide the merits of rival favourites, or to settle the litigations constantly pending between irritated feudatories. When such a state of affairs exists, there can be neither salutary government at home nor trustworthy engagements abroad.

In another point of view, it leaves room for sudden changes, by holding out an occasion to ambitious generals to form an empire of their own out of the surrounding corruption. And indeed it is a very significant fact what skilled connoisseurs these eastern potentates are becoming in the merits of Krupps and Armstrongs.

China has remained under the same rulers for a period of two hundred and thirty years. But if it be true that all history repeats itself, we must arrive at the conclusion that even a dynasty whose ninth representative is on the throne, is not safe from the fate of its predecessors. It is also a fact not to be lost sight of, that, strictly speaking, there is no regular army. The forces correspond more to our militia, residing at their own houses, and not in barracks, and occupying themselves in trades or labour of some kind, except on those special days when they are summoned to their divisions.

Our first attempt to open trade intercourse with China was in 1637, when the East India Company despatched several vessels to Macao ; but through the intrigues of the Portuguese, then as now in possession of that town, the attempt proved a failure, and the ships were forced to depart without effecting their purpose. For more than a century afterwards a limited traffic was carried on with Canton by the East India Company; but the Chinese were never cordial about it, and the Portuguese were not at all chary of spreading reports to our disadvantage. In 1792, however, an embassy was sent under Lord Macartney, to see if some better arrangements could not be concluded, and to bear gifts of friendship from the conquerors of India ; but it is impossible to say the success attending this mission was more than dubious. In 1816 the Earl of Amherst again attempted the hopeless task of pointing out the advantages to be derived from trade and intercommunication, but with no better result than Lord Macartney had met with.

In 1834 the monopoly of the East India Company was abolished, and general traders had the right granted them to transact business with the country. In 1842, after a war in which Canton was much damaged and the Chinese Government had to pay a large indemnity, a treaty of commerce was ratified between Great Britain and China, by which five ports were declared open to English merchants. They were Canton, Amoy, Foo-chow, Ningpo, and Shanghai. Hong-Kong was also ceded to us for ever.

I need not here recapitulate the leading features of the last war, which resulted in the entry into Pekin and the treaty of Tientsin. The events of that war are sufficiently well known, although I may mention that eight more ports were opened to the foreigner, viz., Swatow, Tientsin, Cheefoo, Kiu-Kiang, Hankow, Chin-Kiang, New Chang, and Formosa.

It is notorious that, even after two hundred years of some kind of contact, we are not on as friendly terms as might be, and that all our efforts to break through the phlegm of the Chinaman have been only rewarded with a limited success. We are looked upon as intruders, we are only permitted to remain on sufferance; and whether the future will bring any improvement in these respects is more than the most sanguine of us can answer satisfactorily. At all events, our patience cannot now be complained of, and we have put up for thirteen years with circumstances that have seemed on many occasions about to produce a quarrel. The question, then, changes to, Has our complaisance gone too far in the other direction?

CHAPTER V.

SOME REMARKS ON QUESTIONS SUGGESTED BY OUR INTERCOURSE WITH CHINA.

A SINGLE glance at the map is sufficient to show that the position of China is one entitling it to play a most prominent part in, and to attract much attention from those desirous of participating in, the politics of Asia.

The antiquity of its history, the hardly perceptible difference in the chief characteristics of its inhabitants for thousands of years, the exclusiveness in which it has kept itself aloof from western advances, and the halo of fancy and mystery that surrounds all those things that are little comprehended, combine to make the Celestial Empire an interesting subject. To these, however, must now be added the importance of our commercial relations,— the fact of our being established in settlements on its soil, and, perhaps more than all, the feeling that we are there in keen competition with other nations. It has not been hitherto held an attribute of the English race to draw back from any course for fear of rivals; rather has it been the contrary, and we have carried out many an undertaking merely for the sake of thwarting some opponent. Its reputed history dates from about 2,000 years before the birth of our Saviour. It is thus synonymous i length with that of the Jews empire has passed away nearly 2,000 years, while that of its far eastern contemporary seems to be still, for an Asiatic power, in the full strength of manhood. Through many changes of ruling dynasty, through many a desperate rebellion, through passing under the sway of such conquerors as Genghis Khan, it has come down to our time a relic of the past. We have an ancient people before us, we have the unlimited power of the priesthood, we have the omnipotent majesty of the sovereign enshrined in the hearts of the people. More than this: the wonders of our modern life, what must appear to them the astonishing results of our mechanical appliances, seem to be regarded with a certain apathy and indifference. They nowadays go abroad; but if they do, they carry China with them. They never depart with the idea of no return. They feel satisfied that even if they do die in the strange world they have entered upon, their bodies will be brought back to rest among their forefathers.

It is no part of my object to reconcile the age of the Chinese institutions with the Jewish Cosmogony; but anyone's eyes are sufficient to show him that "Tartar" is written on every lineament of a Chinaman. Whether they be the descendants of Tartaric hordes who in prehistoric times supplanted some aboriginal race, or whether the Tartar bands of Mongolia and Central Asia are the offshoots of an over-redundant population, is to my mind an unimportant question. These Tartars of the desert have, however, a by no means trivial anxiety for the imperial minds at Pekin.

We have seen that their irruptions have been frequent, that they have left a permanent mark in many of the institutions of the country, that they have not a few times furnished a ruler to the empire, and that the present sovereigns are their descendants. Against these intruders an immense and fortified wall was erected. That wall, even if it may seem antiquated to our eyes, and utterly trivial in these days of rifled ordnance, has for centuries been regarded as one of the wonders of the world; and might even on a future occasion form a by no means unimportant opposition to the attack of anyone in that direction. Its safest defence on this side is, however, the character of the obstacles the immense extent of that northern part of Asia offer to anyone who should wish to march an army on that quarter. The south-west of China is also almost totally unexplored, although it seemed, a short time ago, that at last this desirable object was to be accomplished by an expedition starting from Rangoon. It is well known how that attempt resulted in failure, and the murder of a most promising official.

A quarter of a century ago, it was prognosticated that China was to be a new El Dorado; and although those expectations have been only realized in a limited degree, we cannot say that we have exhausted every means to accomplish that end. As yet the iron horse has not ploughed up the land; the rivers and canals are still traversed by the heavy-rigged barges, and news still travels with the tortoise pace of the courier. Each province, each village, must rest therefore on its own resources in any emergency that may arise. But yet, as a sign of the wealth of the country, we have a population which in certain districts is truly immense. The national thrift of course accounts for this in some degree. The real secret, perhaps, of its wealth, is, however, the number and size of its rivers. In the centre there is the majestic Yangtse-Kiang; in the north there is the equally imposing

Ho-ang-Ho; while in the south there is the no less useful Kiu-Kiang.

These highways given by nature perforate the country in all directions. Not only is the land copiously irrigated, but these means of communication require no paternal and careful legislature to keep them in permanent order. Our chief informants on every point of Chinese custom and history—the Jesuits—dwell on the importance of this fact, and many have carefully and eloquently detailed the immense advantage of these splendid streams.

Père Mailla, in his "Histoire Generale de la Chine," which is a French translation of the orthodox Chinese History, which I believe he was also chiefly instrumental in compiling in the reign of Kang-hi, gives a most vivid description of the whole country, in which he resided for a great number of years. No further information, I may say, has been added to that he affords us, and the history of the Celestial Empire has yet to be written. Her bold and extensive seaboard, stretching for hundreds of miles, from which not even the horrors of the typhoon can detract its many advantages, is specially intended for the children of commerce; and although it may seem a paradox, the supposition is not opposed by the facts.

The leading merchants along the Straits of Malacca are, if not Chinese by birth, certainly so by origin, and are distinguished by the term "Baba." Their trade with the Philippine Isles and Cochin China is also extensive, and this is carried on chiefly, if not altogether, in native ships.

The appearance of the Chinese in the labour market of California has been attended with such success that there are some who are sanguine enough to point to a time when demand for their services will be universal. What would not some of our colliery proprietors, and other employers of labour, they say, give for workmen who would be content with a fair and fixed wage, and with no inducement or wish to strike for higher terms; and these all the time no unskilled, incapable persons;— persons who have proved themselves most adaptable to strange surroundings; steady, sober; if humoured in some of their religious and superstitious observances, most amenable to authority? If we may despise many of their characteristics as meannesses; if we prefer to pride ourselves on our openness of character, let us not forget that the reasons for which we contemn them are the very ones that would render them most valuable in any civilized country which may at present be agitated to its heart's core by the difficulty of obtaining men, and by the antagonism, every day becoming more embittered, between capital and labour. The thousands who annually arrive on the shores of California are so many proofs that there would be no impossibility in attracting them from their own country. Australia also is visited by a considerable number. These emigrants, of whom the great majority ultimately return to their own country, have also another significance for us. New ideas on the white nations must be springing up in the minds of the natives. The wondrous tales brought back, if viewed with apathy and unconcern, must have some effect, and must leave some impression on their minds. The presence of ambassadors at the capital; the right of audience, so lately conceded; the sight of our men-of-war in their rivers; the remembrances of our prowess; and more than all, perhaps, the knowledge that it was to English officers they owed the suppression of the most formidable rebellion that had disturbed their tranquility for ages, the severity of which is even now brought vividly before them by the sight of the jungle growing where once was the temple, and the silent street where of yore trod the noisy throng,—all these must be taken as being productive of a gradual awakening to the realities of civilization; and if it does not mean any real adoption of our system, it at all events means toleration of it. Indeed, with a power like Russia roaming about somewhere on her northern frontier; with the English and Americans—not to speak of other nations—establishing themselves in her seaports; with free trade openly proclaimed; and, more than all, with a neighbouring and rival power showing an inclination to compete for European popularity, there seem certainly sufficient topics to make even the most conservative of Chinamen desirous of knowing something from whence these audacious interlopers spring. At the same time, they are also bound to confess that to a great degree they are the most benefited by the connexion. There, therefore, can be no doubt that the interior of China will not for much longer continue a *terra incognita;* and although before she fully opens herself to the foreigner complications of a lesser or greater seriousness may arise, they cannot retard the result for long.

In our dealings, political and otherwise, we should always remember that the rule with all eastern nations applies with double force to them, viz., that the slightest hesitation is construed as weakness; and that the only true way of discomfiting their chicanery is an honourable firmness, quick in conception and unflinching in execution.

They are perfectly aware of the jealousies between the different nations trading with them, and are only too alive to the means of setting them by the ears with one another. We are no longer able, as in the last century, to compel the acknowledgment by the natives of our pre-eminence by thrashing all our rivals. We cannot do as Clive did,—conquer India by overcoming Dupleix. So if we are debarred from the simplest solution of the difficulty, it behoves us to be most careful, and to meet all artifices by that most powerful of all policies, firm and truthful candour. Our interests in China are most important; and should the proposed coal investigations turn out successful, would increase to a very great degree; and therefore we must not permit anyone to oust us in our foremost position there. We must not risk present and future advantages by neglecting any opportunity that may occur.

We are an old power, who may have seen days of higher repute, but at no time was our strength greater or of a more lasting description. So even if we can afford to brook our European position to be questioned, our representatives in the colonies only remember what we were, and, rightly or wrongly, cannot tolerate the remotest idea of competition from any quarter whatsoever.

I would here again draw attention to the late expedition exploratory of South-west China, which left Rangoon under Colonel Browne, for the purpose of urging the necessity for a renewal of the attempt; and indeed it is extremely doubtful how we can start under more favourable auspices, as it will seem but a natural demand that a fresh safe-guard to effect this all-important purpose be one of the first requests on the Government of Pekin, as some atonement for the murder of poor Margary.

It is reported that the capabilities for cotton planting are here most promising and extensive. There is no lack of splendid rivers, nor is there scarcity of labour, and there certainly is not more—and probably rather less—ill-will towards foreigners among the people.

This is our question exclusively. Here lies our real high road to China. The impulse that would be given to friendly relations by the commencement of a trade in these parts would be such as would leave little doubt in the minds of the Chinese who their best and most powerful customers really were. On the sea-coast we have, and must always have, formidable rivals. In this direction there are none to question us. We can follow our own plans with deliberation; and as the natives would equally benefit with ourselves, there can be no doubt of the ultimate success. We might by so doing seem to be entering in a race with Russia, who approaches in the north as we should in the south; but if we draw back we are only permitting another power, with more obstacles to contend against, to approach the common goal alone.

CHAPTER VI.

HONG-KONG.

As I said in a previous chapter, I soon became accustomed to my new surroundings, strange as they at first seemed to me.

Hong-Kong, situated on an island, but including in its jurisdiction the neighbouring peninsula of Kow-Loon, at the mouth of the river Kiu-Kiang, was ceded to the English as long ago as 1841.

Its capacious harbour affords most excellent shelter for our shipping, and is surrounded by a range of hills, one and even two thousand feet in height, which are covered with the beautifully-situated houses of the merchants.

On landing, the coolies plying for hire with chairs surrounded us; and I must say on entering one, I found to my surprise that they walked so well together that the journey was not only done very fast, but also in the greatest comfort. Sometimes you unfortunately may, however, get unevenly matched carriers, when the sensation is anything but agreeable. The streets have a very busy look, what with coolies along the Praya, or quay, carrying bales of stuffs, and the general bustling about of the men of commerce. There are several very fine buildings, notably the club, near which is the town-hall. At the club there is a very fair library. All the chief papers arrive by each mail—*Times*, *Pall Mall Gazette*, *Graphic*, *Punch*, etc.; and there is some accommodation for sleepers. There are boat-houses, cricket fields, baths, and racquet courts, where all the great games of old England are to be seen as much enjoyed as on any public ground at home.

The evening I was here on this occasion we had a pleasant drive to Happy Valley, which is the popular resort, and also where the races are periodically held. The road there is a most lively sight,—quite a miniature Rotten Row in a less grand degree: the whole way thronged with all kinds of traps, driven by all kinds of horses, —Australian, China ponies, Manilla ponies, half-breds and thorough-breds, of all hues and of all ages.

I have detailed the various amusements at the service of a resident in Hong-Kong, —which in this instance may be taken as a type of the rest of English life in China,— because nothing struck me more in our countrymen out there than the little desire they showed to return home. At first this surprised me very much; but when I saw the quantity of means at their disposal of passing their leisure pleasantly, the equality in their positions, the sumptuousness, I may term it, of their diet, and the *dolce far niente* of their whole life, my surprise ceased, and my own ideas soon became the same.

Who would compare to this the drudging existence in a London house, the harassing anxiety of an English career, the impossibility of enjoying to any similar degree the comforts of life, and the feeling of the inequality of social status so constantly brought before us in most disagreeable ways? On the one hand, we have every present requirement, with much future hope; on the other, we have monotonous and heart-wearying toil, with an almost barren prospect. But now that I have been compelled to turn my back on this bright prospect, I am able to see that life in China makes self, a god everywhere, the only one. One's moral character suffers for the sake of his material welfare.

The latest news, both of worldly and of private interest, arriving now so regularly and so frequently, makes life abroad much less irksome and tedious than formerly. The Chinese boys who serve as valets are remarkably sharp, and as faithful as any Chinaman can be. They are also so attentive to you, that when giving a dinner they have the bad tact to wait upon yourself in a marked degree, more than on your guests. This has become such an acknowledged fact, that each one brings his own boy. The pidgin English which they speak is often very difficult to understand, and besides, they never get much beyond the pidgin part of it. "Pidgin" means "business," and is used in such idioms as "What pidgin have you done to-day?" My only night here

I used mosquitoe curtains, but as I went to bed late, and had to be up early to catch the river steamer, these tormentors hadn't much time to be a nuisance. The river packets, which ply daily between Canton and Hong-Kong, are very fine steamers—American built—painted white all over. They have three decks; one for the Chinese, one for the passengers, and a small one above for the captain and pilot. The trip takes from six to eight hours, but varies according to the tide.

The river Kiu-Kiang (called here, however, by us, Bocca Tigris, or the Bogue) is very broad, dotted over with islands; but the whole scenery, although pretty, is very flat. Cultivated fields stretch for miles along the banks on either side of the river, with a small range of hills in the distance, and nearer at hand a pagoda or two ever and anon peeping out from over the foliage.

The whole view was pleasant and homely looking.

We stopped at Whampoa, a few miles from Canton, where all ships with merchandise are loaded, as they cannot proceed up to Canton. The river, and in fact all, steamers, however, can go up to the town; but sailing ships never proceed higher than Whampoa. From here I could distinctly see Canton, with the French Cathedral towering above the houses. The whole place seemed a plain of roofs, with here and there a lofty narrow house rising through the gloom, which are either places to look out for fires, or pawn-shops where most Chinese place their winter clothes, furs, etc., to be taken care of; things which, if kept without extra precaution, would spoil during the summer. The loss, however, entailed by fire is sometimes very severe on individuals, and very widely felt; the liability of the care-takers being not at all legally established. The Government derives a large revenue from shops, particularly pawn-shops.

On coming up the river through the town, we passed through the city of Sampans, or boats. These, packed closely together, lay stretched on either side of me. The numbers who dwell in these cannot be at all accurately estimated, and add greatly to the difficulty of even approximating to the population of Canton. The banks of the river, on approaching the city, are lined with pretty little houses, inhabited by well-to-do Chinamen. These have nice little gardens running down to the banks of the river, with a little boat lying at its anchorage. Then we saw the houses of the missionaries—nearly all French—quite surrounded by the native settlements. This used to be the old factory site before the war. Then there is Honam, which at one time was a favourite locality for foreigners; but since Shameen has been built, it has been deserted by all except Parsee merchants or Portuguese clerks, with the Chinese tea manufactories; so that all the English houses, or Hongs, with one exception alone, do their business in the settlement, but have to go to Honam to weigh their teas previous to shipment.

On reaching the wharf, which was thronged with Chinese, I changed to the house-boat which awaited me, and I was rowed up the river to Shameen, the settlement. It would have been almost impossible, and a most tedious undertaking, to have attempted to have gone through the streets, owing to their narrowness, and to the offensive smells prevalent in all Chinese cities. The river is very broad, and the view of the country on the opposite side of the river, with hardly any houses to intercept it, is pretty.

Shameen, originally a mud flat, was, by a stipulation of the treaty after the last war, made, at the Chinese Government's expense, into a settlement for foreigners. The little island is walled all round with a quay, or rampart, to protect it from the river, and also as some means of keeping the damp out. The top of this is paved with chunam—a kind of asphalte—and being bordered with trees, short though bushy, forms an agreeable promenade, where many a pleasant walk have I enjoyed in the evening. It is known by the name of the Bund. I called Shameen a little island, it being divided from the native town at the back by a canal called the Creek, but is connected with the mainland by bridges, at each of which a native policeman is always stationed to enquire the business of every native who wants to enter. The other side is facing the open river, so that the shape of the island is very similar to that of an egg. In size it is about one and a half miles round. Chinese gunboats, commanded by foreigners, are also stationed opposite the island, for the better protection of the residents. Two long rows of houses—although not quite over the whole extent of the island, as the French part is not inhabited—run across it. The settlement is so loved by all, that it is often called the Paradise, as everything is supposed to be nearly perfection, all the residents being regarded as fellow-members of one large family, from which the backbiting and scandal so rife in small communities is supposed to have been entirely banished. The roads are of grass, with beautiful avenues of trees; outside these are good paths of chunam. There is also a small flower garden, where the children play. Within the last two years a capital hall has been erected, with a stage and theatre. This is also used very often for dances. Adjoining is a good bowling-alley.

The first night I arrived, there happened to be a ball given by a resident before returning to England. As the night was wet, we had chairs round after dinner to take us there. Outside the building there was quite a posse of chair-coolies, all in different costumes, holding lanterns with the names of their masters in Chinese and English. The whole looked fantastic and somewhat weird. The entrance was decorated with much taste, and everything was admirably got up. The great drawback was of course the scarcity of ladies, many having to dance with two or three gentlemen for one dance.

No one drives in Shameen, but many keep their ponies for riding in the evening, although there is such limited space for horse exercise. There are a racquet court, boat-houses, and club, the last of which contains billiard and reading-rooms. The markers at the tables are Chinese boys, many of whom play a good game. Picnics, which are quite the rage, are often got up,—when prettily decorated boats are called into requisition to convey gay parties up and down the river to their destination. Some of these are able to go up little creeks where rowing is impossible; and often in these pretty retreats comfortable places can be found to enjoy the capital lunch always provided for such occasions. And it has been my good fortune to have shared in several of these expeditions, when, beneath a tasty rustic bridge, and with music from a neighbouring temple breaking soothingly upon the ear, I have done ample justice to game pies and champagne.

Shameen's Local Government Board is a council elected by the residents, and each member looks after a department; *e.g.*, one takes the police, another the roads, another something else, and so on. The contrast this pleasant retreat bears to the great bustling native city is soothing and tranquilizing. But the social ties are no less imposing there than in our civilized communities. The round of visits obligatory on all new arrivals no sooner ceases, than the round of dinners-out succeeds, and keeps the martyrdom up.

Two or three days after my arrival, I took chairs to go to see our consul, Sir Brooke Robertson, who resides through the native city, at a place called the Yamen. This was a most tedious and awful journey, the streets being too narrow to admit of more than one chair passing at a time, and the roofs of the houses nearly meet across the street. Whenever we encountered another chair, we had to stand aside somehow or other, and let it squeeze past. On my way we were caught in a storm, the rain coming down in torrents, —so much so that although my bearers toiled on knee-deep in it for some time, they at last were forced to take shelter in the court of a temple, where I was in close proximity to one or two life-size gods. There were also many of the poorer Chinese sheltering here, who could not restrain their curiosity, but now and then pulled my curtains aside and had a peep at me. All this made me a little nervous, and by energetic signs I made the coolies, who couldn't understand even pidgin English, go on again, although they had still to wade knee-deep. After more than an hour's journey we reached the Yamen. This proved to be a delightful place, quite *à la chinoise*,—fine park with deer, and a pond in front of the house. The fourth side of each room is a verandah, and everything very comfortable and nice: the whole place surrounded by magnificent trees, and about the grounds lie some ruins, mementoes of the last war. From a tower here I had a splendid view of the country.

The French consul lives somewhere near, but isolated as it is among natives who certainly under present circumstances don't want much incentive to become vindictive and blood-thirsty, it seemed to me anything but a pleasant locality to reside in. Sir Brooke Robertson, however, said he liked the quiet very much, and employed most of his leisure in reading.

I was very glad to get back to the settlement, as this was my first expedition into the native quarters; and if my bearers had deserted me, as at any moment they might have, I should have found it utterly impossible to get out of a maze where right and left, before and behind, had exactly the same appearance, and as I could not speak the language it would have been impossible for me to discover my road by enquiry.

The beggars in the streets were a most horrible sight, and I was told that they live to a great extent on the vermin off their bodies. This is almost too disgusting to be put on paper.

My impressions of a Chinese city from this journey were anything but prepossessing. The inconvenience owing to the narrow streets, the offensive smells, the disagreeableness of being brought into close contact with such disgusting sights as these outcasts, make a visit to the native quarters no pleasant task, and one seldom wished to be quickly repeated. To get into one's bath, and shake off the contamination, was a relief, and to seek as quickly as possible forgetfulness in rational comforts and intercourse with others of the knowledge of what the human race can become through generations of neglect and misfortune, through squalor, misery, and poverty, of a kind that is beyond even the comprehension of a East London Samaritan.

CHAPTER VII.

CANTON.

CANTON, the chief town and residence of the Governor of the province of Quang-Tung, was the first port, and for a long time the most important one, with which the English carried on trade intercourse; although it has of late years—since the great destruction in Canton during the war—been eclipsed by its younger rivals, Shanghai and Foo-Chow, which enjoy the special advantage of having greater facilities of reaching the tea plantations.

Canton, however, besides being an important place on account of its commerce, is also, it must not be forgotten, a great

Chinese city, and the multitude of barges and boats that proceed up country are so many instances of the activity and importance of its inland trade. Its population has been estimated at various figures, some patently exaggerated, and all, owing to the difficulties attending a census, founded on insufficient evidence.

It is situated on the Kiu-Kiang, which, however, has several other names. It is here a fine broad river; but to all intents and purposes Whampoa is its seaport, it being impossible for sailing ships to come up the river to load, owing to the shallowness of the river. It, therefore, labours under this other disadvantage as compared with its rivals; which can alone be obviated by the construction of a railway between Whampoa and Canton. Permission might be obtained from the viceroy of Quang-Tung, as the Chinese merchants themselves would join in advocating for this local improvement. The funds could easily be raised, and as there would be no national opposition, the undertaking would not run much risk, especially if the promoters were content to commence with a tramway, to prepare the popular mind for the more formidable appearance of the steam engine.

Canton, lying in a plain, is surrounded on the north by a long range of hills called the Pak-Wan, or White Cloud, Mountains. They are very barren, and are used as the cemetery of the city. These attain some elevation, and are situate about seven or eight miles from the walls by which the city is surrounded. The walls are about seven miles in circuit, and form an excellent walking ground, the perambulation of them being the usual preparation for our Sunday dinner. Outside the walls are canals, which are a most disgusting sight when the tide is out. The view of the surrounding scenery is good, and from some of the pagodas situate on them the prospect is very pretty.

The principal streets, for a native town, are considered to be clean, although now and then the odour is most offensive. Curio Street, one of the best, is the place for curio and china shops. Some of these are very fine, and are got up in the most magnificent style, with polished panelling and gilding freely all round, and with a sort of bower for the sellers to sit in. Some are so extensive as to have three or four floors covered with most exquisite china. However, in the curio shops particularly, one has to bargain greatly, as the prices demanded are most exorbitant. The better shops are, however, beginning to have fixed and tolerably reasonable prices marked on their wares; and this good example is being imitated to some degree by all. Hoa Ching, the great ivory carver, who obtained honourable mention at the Vienna Exhibition, has a shop here; but he has little ready-made fine carving, so everything has to be ordered, often taking from three to four years before it is executed. In hot weather visiting these shops is like going into an oven.

Canal Road is a newer street that Curio Street, but even these fine and chief streets are quite narrow, and transit is a matter of much difficulty. Most of the houses are only two stories high, and there are few buildings that attract much attention for their external appearance. Some of the joss houses, or temples, are extensive; one at Honam in particular, covering several acres. These are not only the temple of the god, but the residence and cemetery of his priests. There is a part of the city set specially aside for lepers, bearing the name of the Leper City; and the Chinese also seem to suffer to a remarkable degree from stone. It is no unusual sight to see in boats, which however must keep away from others, persons suffering from leprosy, who are fearful and disgusting objects. I forgot to mention that another disadvantage from the shops being so close to one another is that the passengers in the streets receive the benefit of the mixture of smells, which is anything but pleasant.

It is a difficult matter to distinguish between the social ranks at a glance; but as a general rule the short coat means inferiority and the long coat superiority. For instance, our "boys," on going home for a holiday, always put on their long coats, to show they still retained their old social position, and out of deference to their parents; and some of the hongs, or foreign houses, had the tact to perceive this trait, and made them appear in long coats when waiting at table; but strange to say, for another reason, they have an objection to this, as the short coat is more comfortable to work in. It is by humouring inferior nations in their superstitious and social observances that we can alone hope to gain their affection. Tact and apparent sympathy gain hearts and good opinion all the world over. The coolies' or labouring man's ordinary apparel is pajamah-trowsers and a short tunic made of a brown material, with an oily appearance much like the canvas stuff worn by fishermen at our ports. Their whole appearance and conduct is quiet, and impresses one favourably after the rowdyism and dissipation of our large towns. They seem to treat their families well, and if not violently affectionate, are at least considerate in their actions with their own. The merchant classes have the same characteristics, and show themselves to be certainly our equals, if not superiors, in all matters of commercial diplomacy. Many proofs of this will be adduced in the course of this narrative, and will be of more service and easier to supply than any specified examples of this fact. The Chinaman is remarkably civil and obliging in his manner, except when eating. It is then no easy task to get him away from his meal of rice—which is generally flavoured with some greasy substance; but at all other times no fault can be found with his temper. It is that precious quality that makes him such a formidable customer to deal with, and few of the arts of plausibility are unknown to either the shopkeeper or the merchant.

The women are allowed a considerable

amount of liberty, although of course it is well known that Chinese ladies never walk abroad. Their feet are therefore remarkably small; and rivalry among beauties is decided by a comparison of their extremities. They have to be carried from their houses to their chairs, in which they alone go about. But this they are allowed to do, I may say, without any further escort than their bearers. As, however, they are curtained in most carefully, there is no real breach of Eastern etiquette. Their ordinary costume is silk pajamahs and beautifully embroidered white jackets. They wear their hair brushed up, with numerous pins in it, and they ornament themselves most tastefully with flowers,—some even putting exquisite little ones in their ears as earrings.

When one gets a little accustomed to their features, many points of merit and attraction are visible in them, far more so than any Englishman is at first willing to admit. Little is known of their internal and domestic relations. I never heard of any instance of a white man obtaining to any degree of intimacy in a native family, although there are many foreigners in the Government's employ; still they always are kept a race apart, and their own pride assists the native reserve. It is, therefore, no unusual thing to meet men who have lived a lifetime in China with scarcely any knowledge either of their social customs or of their personal character, beyond business matters. There are even cases of men who have never gone into Chinese quarters since the time when they went for curiosity during the first months of their arrival out there. They are content to live on in the settlement, to be ignorant of the place where they really dwell, or at the farthest to accept second-hand information that may at any time have a most important bearing on their own affairs; and to divide their existence into three parts—their business, their meals, and their sleep. These have a great deal to do with the antipathy of the natives to foreigners. They have never endeavoured, or done anything whatever, to meet the race objections of those with whom they were compelling an intercourse. On the contrary, their manner and arrogance have on many occasions caused more offence; and when tact and some fellow-feeling would have smoothed over many a difficulty, they have blunderingly made matters worse by a harsh and off-handed interference.

Of course there have been exceptions; there have been some wiser than their generation, and the gratitude of the whole community out there is due to their praiseworthy efforts. Principally for these reasons the Jesuits are alone versed in the details of real Chinese life; but as they openly aim at converting them, they raise such powerful enemies that the reward of their tact and good management is perverted for another reason.

One of the chief reasons why, when the Chinese Government came to look upon trade with foreigners as a necessary evil, they appointed Canton as the port, was its distance from Pekin.

Canton, although in the same latitude as Bengal, enjoys a much milder climate, and never attains to the immense heat of India. Snow has been known to stay some hours on the ground, although it is reported the natives were then ignorant of its name. The learned professions are very numerous throughout the empire; but it seemed to me that the power and wealth lay more in the hands of the military and merchant classes. The *Pekin Gazette*, which appears every day, and in which all the imperial edicts and ordinances—even the most trivial—are promulgated, is a most important and powerful machine of tyranny. It would be strange if, as is suggested by some, we should borrow from a Chinese institution the idea of starting a similar daily official paper. We see there its power, the influence it unavoidably has on men's minds; and if in our case it could not be made the assistant of tyranny, it certainly would, if only to a slight degree, be made the partisan and supporter of a party ministry. Interpreters of the *Gazette* form a regular profession throughout China, and answer in some way to the improvisatori of Italy. This paper is only a production of the merest court trifles, and everything is viewed in the light of that clique who for the time being may be foremost in the councils at Pekin. It is, therefore, no reliable exponent of the nation's sentiments, and it is in no way to be trusted in our dealings with the country at large.

CHAPTER VIII.

RESIDENCE IN CANTON.

On the opposite side of the river, which is here about four hundred yards across, and almost facing the "settlement," are some very pretty flower and nursery gardens, known by the name of Fa Tie. All the flowers for dinner tables and general use are obtained here. The head boy or butler makes all the arrangements for the supply, which is done at a contract price; and as flowers are so extensively used for ornament, this is a very heavy item in the bills, and generally turns out a good thing for the contractor. The lotus flower, worn so much by the native girls in their hair, is perhaps the most conspicuous; but there are also small shrubs, trained over wire in pots, and fantastically interwoven into all sorts of designs, such as foreigners in boots, trowsers, and tall hats, or dogs, huts, etc. Remarkable taste is shown in the blending of colours, and the workmanship in executing the design is highly artistic, and is all done by native workmen. These gardens are a very nice place to stroll in on a Sunday evening before dinner, having also a row there and back.

The Hong with which I was being the only one that transacted their business at Honam, I enjoyed a pleasant pull every morning and evening. All the other Hongs do their work in the settlement, only going to Honam to weigh the teas. The customs are collected at Canton by Europeans, and they form an extensive establishment, supervised by Commissioners. There are also interpreters attached to the staff; but with none of these did I come much in contact, as they reside in a large building in the city, near the Custom House. As an instance of the little inducement to anyone to go about and investigate the place, a globe trotter—such is the name given to a traveller—whom I had under my care to show about the city, was so overcome by the smells and heat, that after the first day he refused to stir beyond the house.

Some little way down the river there are tea gardens; at least they are called so, as there are a few tea shrubs here. Of course it is generally known that Canton itself is not a tea district. Here one can get a capital country walk,—although, of course, there are no roads, only small paths made by the labourers; and, consequently, it is as rough work as on a highland moor;—the whole place quite open, and no boundaries visible;—a patch of something grown here and there, a clump of trees, and all the rest a wide, open, untilled, uncultivated plain, swarming with buffaloes, on which the people ride. As these animals hate a white face, and often rushed at us, we had to keep on the alert, and several times had to place a ditch between them and ourselves. This was great fun.

The country people are very civil, allowing us to go anywhere, so long as we didn't touch their crops, and to shoot anything we saw. They seemed very good-tempered and not at all ill-disposed towards us; only just a little bit curious.

We took a photograph, and stuck it up as a target to shoot at, to show them what we could do, and also to amuse them. After riddling it considerably we gave it to them, making them understand it was our likeness; at which they rushed away with it in great excitement, thinking they had got a prize.

We met altogether a good many labourers, and from none received any incivility whatever, all kow-towing to us in the most courteous manner, and we doing the same in return. It was very pleasant to see them so friendly disposed, and I really believe the people themselves have no such bad feeling towards us as is the received opinion. Their priests and rulers for their own motives and advantage stir them up against foreigners, availing themselves of the popular superstitions and fearful ignorance of the masses to prejudice them against all advances from Europeans. They have really been kept in leading-strings ever since our intercourse with the country has been looked upon as an imminent danger by the ruling powers. But this cannot be done much longer. The people must soon begin to feel their own importance and real power, and then wish to have some voice in the matter; and then we shall find that, imperceptibly it may be at first, their opinion differs to a very considerable degree to that enunciated for them heretofore by persons who arrogate to themselves the right to dictate their line of conduct in every important question.

This feeling of hostility to strangers has been fostered and greatly supported by the zeal of missionaries, who, if they have been the forerunners in many instances of the settler, have also never assisted the settler in overcoming the repugnance all natives feel at the forcible adoption of their country as a home by foreigners. They have always drawn the fierce polemics of religion into a question that should be decided by reciprocal benefits alone. There is time enough to convert them when our higher system of life has fixed itself on their imagination. Man has too often been proved to be only influenced by material considerations to permit of any doubt of this assertion; and he is in that the same, if in nothing else, whether black or white, whether bond or free.

The Jesuits, who are the chief missionaries in China, have adopted the dress and external appearance of the inhabitants, in order to pass the better unnoticed in native quarters, into which they venture with a careless recklessness. They have even imitated the national pigtail. Some of them live in huts in the mountains as hermits, and acquire great reputations for holiness, and also for skill and power as curers of illnesses, although the national doctor is ceaseless prayer alone.

One day we started, a party of five, in a

yacht early in the morning to go up the river for a little trip. These yachts are somewhat expensive, costing from £180 to £200, although a native-built boat to answer every necessary purpose can be got for about £40 to £60. The expensive yachts are most comfortable, with a good saloon large enough for six to sit down to dinner, a ladies' cabin, a lavatory, and a cooking place for the boys to prepare a meal. These are generally used only by two men, who go away for two or three weeks' shooting; but this is done more particularly in the north, where the sport is better. Down south we still had the satisfaction of receiving some of their spoil in the shape of immense game pies.

The yachts in question are worked by about six sailors. On this occasion we were unfortunate in having no wind, so that we were only able to go up about twenty-four miles. The scenery was most lovely, with pagodas on the tops of the hills, villages delightfully situated and half-hidden by trees,—the whole reminding me very much of the Rhine, only, of course, not quite so elevated. We came to a place called Kum Shan, where as you turn a corner you see a very high range of hills looking very black and formidable; and the river here seems to abruptly terminate, or to go under the mountains.

Here we were caught in one of those fearful storms which are of frequent and sudden occurrence, so that accidents take place tolerably often; the boats being worked only with one sail, capsize very easily. We took shelter under the shore; but the moment it abated, we availed ourselves of the wind to return, as it might fail us at any moment, and we did not wish to sleep in the boat.

One of the most curious sights was the

mode adopted along the river of irrigating the country. As the banks are much higher than the river, every hundred yards or so two men, standing on a sort of wooden platform, tread away for hard life with a trough running down into the water, up which the water was drawn by means of these men treading and working a long sort of paddle-wheel. The water is thus thrown up on the land, and flows through the country in dykes. Sometimes there were even five or six men working, and all the time under a blazing sun.

We met many boats rowed by women; the chief point about these being that they wear one long plait down their back, with their hair cut short across their foreheads, which is different to the usual custom, as I explained before. These boat-women, tanned to a darker colour, had not at all a prepossessing appearance, and resembled to a great degree those unfortunate beings who ply a similar livelihood in barges on our own canals.

Many petty acts of theft are committed daily; for instance, one of us had been losing jewellery to some extent, and we told the head boy or butler that he must discover the culprit, or we should hold him responsible for the loss. At this he was in a great fright, but still the thief could not be discovered. After several more things being taken, one of the boys disappeared; so we sent the chief detective—a very clever fellow—after him; and with a little difficulty he found him in a gambling-house,— to which all the Chinese when they get a little money resort: but when he heard that the detective was coming, he stabbed himself twice in the stomach, to save himself from the thrashing with the bamboo he would have got at the Yamen, which is the punishment for theft. He was sensible enough not to hurt himself very much, as all I heard of him afterwards was that he was continually getting better. The head butler was held responsible, and had to make up for the losses. The custom is, when he engages the boys he takes the risk of any loss that may occur through them.

As an instance of their extreme love of spirits, this fellow had a bad leg, and was given at his request a bottle of fine Cognac to bathe it with. This did him so much good that he wanted another; when he had had three, however, he was given a case of common stuff brought from Hong-Kong. This, however, he returned with proud indignation, declaring it was not the good sort. This made us quite certain where the first bottles had gone, and, as we didn't want the poor fellow to become a confirmed toper, he got no more.

The natives are much given to imbibing spirits on every opportunity, and their own favourite beverage, samshu, is a most powerful stimulant distilled from rice.

CHAPTER IX.

RELIGIOUS CEREMONIES.

There is no special day in China, like our Sunday, for universal prayer and rest; but the festival and other holy days are quite sufficient in number to make up for this deficiency. The great festival I saw while out there was the Dragon Festival. This is one of the chief public celebrations, and preparations are made for it weeks before its coming off. The performers in it go in for a course of training just as we do for our boat races and other athletic sports. The principal part of the ceremony consists in processions of boats up and down the river. These boats, although often capable of containing eighty or ninety persons, are only just wide enough to admit of one sitting down; so anyone can easily imagine what a length they must be when they carry nearly a hundred people. The wonder is that there are not more frequent accidents through upsets. Each of the rowers has a little paddle, which he dips into the water very quickly, thus propelling the boat along at a good pace. The handles, which they hold with both hands, are so short that in paddling they almost touch the water with their hands. Most, being well trained, keep capital time. A man standing in the bow of the boat with a sort of a wand in his hand, waving it from side to side, invokes the spirit of the river to give them back some great sage who lived long ago, and who conferred great benefits upon his countrymen—I do not think it was Confucius;

but others say this man in the bow of the boat is supposed to be distributing corn, etc., to the river, and praying that a good and prosperous harvest may be vouchsafed to them. There are several other legends attached to this proceeding. Between the rowers stand men beating gongs and playing other instruments, and there is an elaborately decorated altar in the middle, with men holding large silk banners around it. All the men standing up are dressed in yellow silk coats, fantastic hats, and blue or red trowsers; and I have been told that these have a very high opinion of themselves ever after, from having held such a post of honour in this day's festivities. The noise from the gongs, which are continually kept going, is something fearful, and can be heard quite distinctly half a mile off. In this way they go on all day, going up and down the river. All the Chinese flock to the river banks, and the rival merits of the boats are as much the topic of conversation and difference of opinion as is the case at any of our own national amusements and public events. On this day we permit them to come on to the settlement, as the best view is obtained from there; but when it was all over we were only too glad to get rid of them, although they behaved themselves remarkably well, and we could find nothing to complain of. Still, we had to keep ourselves in all day, not to give them any inducement, with their religious frenzy about them, of making a row. Before permission was given them, it was mooted that it might be advisable to request the Chinese Viceroy to send some military on the island for that day, as an extra precaution. This was not, however, after careful consideration, deemed to be necessary. So with this extra reason for doubt in our minds, we were greatly rejoiced at their departure. I felt myself inclined to question the wisdom of permitting their admittance, thinking that it would appear more a right than an obligation to them, and at the same time excite jealousy by the general appearance of the wealth of the settlement.

About the same time I saw another very pretty sight on the river—the feast in honour of the departed, which continued for several nights. Immense boats are hired for this occasion, and covered with lighted lanterns. These are hung round the boat, and the masts are lit up with them, and triangles and all sorts of arches are formed by these slung on ropes all over the boat. The richer Chinamen give splendid dinners on board to their friends, with lots of music and beautiful girls to dance and wait upon them. Each of their boats, too, have kites and balloons, with variegated lamps attached to them, and there are crowds of these boats in all parts of the river; but the principal place is at the flower boats, or the regular streets of boats, which are always stationary, and where all the Chinese dinners are given. The river during this season has a very gay appearance, as can be well imagined. Oil is burnt in the lamps, as well as I could find out, and the oil bill is one of the heaviest household items in a family, owing to the native boys stealing it in such quantities. They take it home to their people, who flavour their food with it.

One day while out rowing in a four oared boat, we came across some of these fellows practising, on the occasion of the Dragon Festival, in their long boats. On our coming up to them they raced alongside, and worked themselves into a tremendous fit of good-tempered excitement trying to beat us. But though no one would believe it when we mentioned it, we beat them, though not without much exertion. They grinned and "Hey-heyed" us the whole way, but took their defeat in perfect temper, and "Kow-towed" us on our leaving them. I did not see any more festivals, but often met great processions in the street returning from something of the sort; but beyond delaying us in getting along, as they took up most of the room, they seemed too engrossed in their own antics to bestow any of their attention on foreigners. So there is no forced obeisance, as in some Roman Catholic countries is imposed on those who may happen to witness the progress of any of these religious bodies. As far as I could see, all the natives did was to stand still, thus showing their respect. In these processions boys come first, dressed in gaudy attire, with banners and images, and carrying a ginger-bread sort of thing, with probably a joss or god inside; the whole brought up with men clashing cymbals, and playing on other instruments which sound very like the bag-pipes; and indeed the whole procession reminded me most of our Lord Mayor's Show. They, however, did not strike me as being a very religious people, although the superstitious rites and observances seem to have great hold on their minds.

Some of their temples are fine buildings, with exquisite carving on the walls, which are of stone; but the courtyard is the resort of the beggars,—what I may call a Chinese workhouse, or rather casuals ward; and they are only turned out when some religious performance is about to take place.

As I said, the only doctor is prayer. To give an instance of this, when I was at Macao, a tea-boy, who lived with his family in a lodge near our house, was very much afflicted on account of his wife's illness, as she was supposed to be dying. But the only thing to be done, he said, was to call in the priests; and as he lived some distance from the house, permission was given him to have them. The consequence of this to us was that we got little rest that night. But the priests came in and dinned their horrid music round her bed, praying their gods that she might be cured. In this case their prayers were efficacious; but what would any of our doctors say to this noisy pantomime going on in a patient's room? The husband, however, seemed to be somewhat sceptical as to the real cause of his wife's recovery; a scepticism which perhaps was owing to the priests requiring a heavy fee. There, as elsewhere, they don't give their services for nothing. But my friend in this case seemed to be a general free-thinker, and quite a republican in his politics. He ranted no less against the evils of mandarinism than some of our cosmopolitan friends do against the abuses resulting from a landed aristocracy. Only do away with the mandarins, and all would come right. Such was his universal panacea. The Chinese would then adopt our customs, and swear an eternal friendship, if we only allied ourselves with such politicians as my friend, to put down the mandarins. He was particularly partial to England, though he resided in a Portuguese settlement, and was very fond of talking of all our wonderful possessions; but nothing seemed to take his fancy so much as our railways. He told me how, many years ago, an Englishman came to Canton, and laid down a line in a room, and had a miniature engine and carriages running on it; and he invited all the influential Chinamen to come and see his railway. He pointed out to them the advantages of adopting such an improvement, and offered, if they would only obtain the requisite authority, to construct it, and carry out all the arrangements for working the railway when built. Many of the merchants were greatly pleased with the idea, fully perceiving what immense advantage it would be to them, and the country generally; but they were either afraid to ask for, or failed to obtain, the permission of the mandarins and other chiefs; and for some reason or other, which I am not aware of, the whole proposal fell through, and has not since been renewed.

I would here advocate, in as strong terms as I can, the revival of this idea; and I would press on the consideration of every one who feels any interest in the welfare of China, the all-importance of this proposal. Where it would be best to make a commencement, whether from Canton to Whampoa, or somewhere else, I leave to those whom a longer residence in China than mine would authorise to speak with greater authority and wider knowledge. But at all events, on its broad principle of public utility, I submit that the introduction of the steam-engine into China is a by no means unimportant question; and China, ill-cultivated and badly-managed as it is, would, by the introduction of mechanical assistance, make such a rapid progress in wealth, that not only would these undertakings quickly repay their promoters, but be of lasting good to the country at large. It would, doubtless, be a task of some difficulty at first to obtain the consent of the mandarins; but even this opposition, although they esteem such a proposal a direct menace at their own authority, would, in my opinion, be overcome by conciliatory advances. At all events, we cannot assert that it is impossible until we have adopted some means more energetic and pressing to influence their decision than any that have been taken as yet.

Perhaps the question, however, may receive a different and more easy solution. One of the chief Viceroys has just commenced, or is about to, excavations for coal, although it is uncertain how far he may feel inclined to carry them; and it is rumoured that if these turn out successful, he will construct what is represented as an old idea of his—a railway in his own province. This, however, will probably not be to benefit foreign trade, but merely to further his own ambitious designs; so, although a beginning in the right direction, this ought to be no reason for deterring undertakings in other provinces, especially when they are intended for a more legitimate and useful purpose.

CHAPTER X.

SOMETHING ABOUT "TEA."

Considering that I have the privilege to belong to a profession whose special subject is "tea," it may not seem out of place to insert here a chapter on this article; and as my remarks will apply both to the plant on the bush and also as it appears to the consumer in England, what I have to say about it may prove sufficiently interesting.

It is well known that on its first introduction into Europe it became a great luxury, and was only procurable by the very rich, on account of its excessive price. For many years after it was known only to epicures; but in this century its use has greatly increased, and it now is no longer the beverage of the few, but one of the chief household necessaries of the many.

In quite recent years we have had the import duty reduced to a mere trifle; and indeed some desire that it should be passed duty free, as an absolute necessary. This is agitated for chiefly by those who wish to set up as formidable a rival as possible to beer and spirit drinking; but it must not be lost sight of that excess in tea drinking, like excess in everything else, has its evil effects. The present tax on tea is also so moderate, and presses so lightly on everybody, that it might be unwise in a moment of impulse to remove it, when it would become a matter of considerable difficulty to supply its place in as satisfactory a manner.

I will begin by giving a description of the manufacture of tea; but it must first be stated that what I say refers to the mode of procedure in Canton and Macao. In the north, at Hankow and Shanghai, the teas are made up near the tea plantations; but in the south the rough leaf is put into bags and then conveyed down the river to Canton or Macao, where this rough leaf is changed into the household article. This plan has great advantages for the tea-man, or man who manufactures the teas; for, instead of having all the tea made after one fashion, and then giving this stock to his broker to sell to the foreign merchant, as would be the case if he received the tea ready-made from the plantation, he need only make a few pounds as a sample; and then, he is also in a position to judge whether, if he accepted the foreigner's offer, it would repay him to make up the whole of the quantity after the sample at the price offered. Again:

if the style of the sample is not approved of, he can have it altered to suit the foreign merchant, who has to consult what is, or what he may consider to be, the taste of the hour; and indeed that taste, being the opinion of the home consumer, is of a most fickle character, and cannot be relied upon as a fair criterion of real merit. But, on the other hand, if this system has advantages for the tea-man, it places the buyer, or foreign merchant, under some disadvantages, especially the following: the tea-man seldom if ever makes the bulk of the tea equal to the approved of "muster" or sample, and as freight has been taken for it in the meanwhile in the home steamer, it is a difficult matter to throw up the arrangement, and a "cut," or, in plainer language, taking so much off the stipulated price, is never satisfactory. Again: there is another drawback in selecting too soon after manufacture; for the muster having come only perhaps a few minutes before hot from the pan, and its being fresh and powerful from the short interval after the scenting operation, anyone, if at all careless or inexperienced, is apt to be deceived, and jump to a hasty conclusion as to its virtues. For if the scent, though under the circumstances mentioned seeming so powerful and satisfactory, has not been properly instilled (the scenting operation I will explain by and by), it passes off on the journey, and on reaching home has lost all the fine aroma that induced the selection; and the worst of this is, that having lost its scent it is comparatively valueless, as highly scented teas are the most sought for in the market.

The usual mode of proceeding is for a great tea-man, just before or at the commencement of the season, which begins in March and April, to send an experienced *employé* to the tea plantations to contract for the quantity of tea he may desire to purchase; and sometimes this contract is made as it grows on the bushes, sometimes when it has been gathered and has undergone partial drying. In the latter state I believe it is most difficult for a foreigner to discern the real quality of the crop; and the experience and knowledge of even old Chinamen are put to a severe test to find out its real value. When the purchases have been made, the plant, after being packed in bags, is conveyed in barges or junks down to Canton, to be converted into the article of sale. Some of the larger of the foreign firms keep their own factories, and advance or lend to their tea-man large sums of money to contract for tea. This plan has the apparent advantage o enabling the foreigner to have his teas made to his own taste and after his own fashion, and also he can rely with greater assurance on the *bona fides* of his manager in making the bulk uniform to the sample, than if he dealt direct with the natives. But on the other hand there is no inconsiderable risk, as the man may speculate unfortunately, and then much money is lost. Many "hongs" have found this plan so unprofitable as to be compelled to resort to the safer course of purchasing off the open market.

The tea factories in Canton are situated chiefly at Honam, and are large buildings, with only one lofty floor however, which is divided into several rooms, some of which are used for firing the tea, others for sorting, and yet again others for the final operation of weighing and packing. On first entering the building we see the firing room, where there are long ranges of stoves which resemble very much the copper to be found in everyone's back kitchen. A fire burns underneath each in a brick grate, and placed on the top is the pan, made of iron or copper, in a slanting position. It is easier for the coolie to turn the tea when the pan is thus placed.

In an ordinarily-sized factory there are about twenty of these stoves in a range, and to each is attached a coolie, whose duty it is to keep continually turning the leaf round and round the pan; and this operation, aided by the heat of the fire, makes the tea assume the shape and size that may be desired. Of course one firing is not sufficient to effect this object, but several; and after one or two more firings it is passed on to other men, who again fire it, at the same time mixing the scenting-flower with it; and this is the operation that fixes the relative value of all teas. If the flower is mixed when the leaf is half open, and the intermingling is well sustained to the last, the aroma will not only be powerful, but durable. But as this scenting flower costs money, many economise its use, and in that case the tea is only scented on the surface, when although, being fresh, the bouquet may seem powerful, it soon passes off.

We then leave the firing-room, and enter the room for sorting, where hundreds of women are sitting crosslegged on the floor with a basket on either side of them. Some separate the young from the old leaves, or large from the small, in order to make them into the different descriptions so far as name and shape of make decide that question,—all coming, however, from the same plantation or bush even. Others take the scenting-flower from the tea after the firing has been finished. If the flower is found to have lost its power, it is thrown away; but, in any case, the flower is not left in the tea.

In another room, smaller than the others, it undergoes its last firing. In this case it is strewn thinly over a sieve, and placed on a bright charcoal fire. It is then placed in baskets in a heap. When this is finished nothing remains to be done but to hand it over to be weighed, and coolies tread it into boxes containing twenty pounds each.

After these are filled, others solder the tops with lead and a hot piece of iron, to make them perfectly air-tight. Then the marks and descriptions are pasted on, and they are ready for inspection by the foreigner before shipment. These boxes are a well-known ornament in the windows of small grocers at home, and the public, seeing such a veritable Chinese article in the window, argue that the contents must needs be as pure.

There is an export duty payable to the Chinese Government, and before a pass to permit the shipment of the teas will be given, they have to be sent through the Custom House.

All teas are usually scented with a white flower which is grown especially for this purpose; but some teas, especially for the South American market, are scented with a different flower, or, more correctly, a seed, called Chulan, and a few very special ones have been scented with the rose leaf. Some of the native brokers are not only very good judges of tea, but also are versed in the causes of the fluctuations of our own market, and often at favourable opportunities ship teas on their own account through us.

Some little time ago there was considerable discussion in the papers, and some grumbling and surprise was manifested at the fact of Russia absorbing all the fine teas; and assertion was made that the public were most willing to give a long price for the genuine article. If such were the case, it would indeed be surprising if we could not have as much of the fine growth as we desired. It is not very difficult to give a proper explanation of the subject. The Russian and English buyers all hasten to Hankow for the opening of the market, and all are equally able to secure the best chops, provided they are willing to pay the price. Now, as the English market will not pay above a certain price, it is impossible for the buyers for home use to go higher than the price which the consumer will pay and the necessary profits. Whereas for special growths in Russia there is a great demand, and therefore their buyers can bid prices which would be ruinous to any English firm to think of offering. Some English firms do purchase these fine teas at heavy prices; but it is not for the home consumption,—they only enter into competition with Russian firms in the market of that country.

But even labouring under this disadvantage of price, it must not be too hastily supposed that we get no fine teas. The difference between the best of the teas we get and those procured by Russia is such as to make it very difficult for an *uneducated* palate to decide either way; and this difficulty is greatly increased by the fictitious use of milk and sugar. What I mean to say is, that our present mode of using tea kills the real aroma of the plant, and as long as the present custom prevails it would be unwise to attempt to introduce a far more expensive article, which the great majority would consider—and with a certain degree of truth, for the reasons I mention—no better than that previously in use. The invariable practice among retail dealers is to mix the fine teas they may buy with a stronger but infinitely coarser growth, because it is preferred' by families. Strength and not quality is the test of the virtues of one's tea grocer, and a tea that looks thin in the cup is set down as an adulterated article at once. This vitiated taste has been fostered to a great extent by the advertisers of " best tea" at a price at which only very ordinary stuff can be purchased. For the practical purpose of every-day use, and in the persons of the million, there can be little doubt that the really fine growths of tea, if introduced, would only produce dissatisfaction; and that when the taste, if ever, for this beverage arrives at a higher state of culture, the natural consequence will result in our receiving as much as we like of the finer qualities.

The epicure, however, if he be content to discard the accessories of milk and sugar, will certainly, when he has learned to detect the difference, require the more delicate flavour of those growths that at present are monopolized by Russia; but under the most probable event it seems that they will even then be confined to the epicure.

But, for the reasons I have alleged, it is clear that to introduce precipitately these superfine teas to the home market would be to appeal to a public really ignorant of their merits, and the only result would be, loss to the merchant and discontent to the consumer. When the palate of the latter has been educated to detect the difference,—which can only be after he has resolved to give up his present custom of imbibing it,—then there is no doubt whatever but that he can obtain what he desires. He must first appreciate its merits, and then consent to pay a greater sum for the increased pleasure.

CHAPTER XI.

A CHINESE DINNER.

And now let me attempt to give some description of a Chinese dinner, their chief meal, and also one of the most important means at present open to us affording an opportunity of gaining any insight into their customs and character; when in the conviviality of the entertainment they discard some of their reserve, and, if only to a slight extent, show themselves as they appear and act towards one another. It is everywhere the same—if you wish for a favourable occasion to understand a man's feelings, put him in the character of host, and invite yourself to dine with him. You have him at a disadvantage, and render it extremely difficult for him to act a feigned part, as, fettered by the customs of his post, he is compelled by sheer necessity to fall back on his habitude; and it is decidedly your own fault if, as the dinner draws nearer to the "walnuts and the wine," all restraint is not banished, and you have the man as he is. It is impossible, unless in the case of the veriest churl, to remain unsociable through it all. The Chinese, put on their metal in the *rôle* of host, fall short in no detail of the most scrupulous courtesy, and they study the faintest wishes of their guests. They have, moreover, that true breeding that sacrifices much of one's own comfort and practices to the prejudices of those they entertain. And the best sign of the success of their efforts is that, despite the strange surroundings, and not to say the repugnance an European must feel to their repast, it is impossible not to be thoroughly at home with them, and to be able to fraternize with them to a very considerable degree.

The broker who invited me gave me *carte blanche* to bring as many friends as I liked, and to name my own day, so as to place no restraint of a fixed appointment upon my own inclination. He also sent me an address in Chinese characters, which I was to give to our head boatman when we intended to accept the invitation.

Of course this dinner was given at the Flower Boats, which is a name given to certain streets in the boat city. The river where these boats are situated is exceedingly rapid, and if the steersman enters the wrong street, backing out again is very awkward, and the risk is great of being sucked under the surrounding boats.

We, however, managed all right, and

met with no contretemps whatever. We arrived at the house or boat about ten o'clock, where many familiar faces welcomed me and the only friend who accompanied me. These acquaintances were specially asked to meet us, to make the whole thing more pleasant for us than it would have been venturing among utter strangers. On each of these boats is a house of one story, having one room half below the deck and another above it.

These boats moored to each other form a perfect street, and in front of each of the houses is a gravelled path. So the scene is the river avenue forming the road and this path for foot-passengers, which is also made quite a promenade of in the evening by persons who come to listen to the music going on inside the houses. On entering the house a coolie immediately attached himself to each of us to fan us, while others brought tea, nuts,—lychees, etc.,—and cigars, or a pipe of opium. This latter we begged to decline.

It may be as well to mention that these houses are regular dining establishments, each party hiring one for the occasion, and the proprietor provides everything as part of his contract. These dinners for, say ten persons, usually cost from £20 to £25, which is expensive.

Sitting round the room we first entered, at several tables were the singers (girls), who sat rouging their faces and admiring themselves in looking-glasses. They also had cups of tea before them, and smoked in the intervals between singing, which they did in turns, to the accompaniment of stringed instruments, played on this night by two men. The men also sang, but their voices are exactly the same as a woman's, which seemed very strange to me when I first noticed it. I had, however, often remarked this before, as our servants always sang over their work at home.

On first hearing a Chinese song, it seems very monotonous to our ears; but when a little more accustomed to it, it loses much of its discordance, and becomes quite endurable and even pleasing. Some of their ballads are very plaintive, and there is even some harmony in their arrangement.

These singers were dressed most beautifully, some even having on magnificent jewellery; while the painting of their faces and the pencilling of their eyebrows, which they perform themselves, were executed most artistically. Perhaps the most striking part of their attire was the splendour of the flowers in their hair. Their hands and fingers are perfection in shape; and they allow one or two of their nails to grow to a great length, as a sign of their owner's pretensions to beauty. But of course there is nothing wonderful in the elegance of their hands, as they do no work of any kind whatever.

None of them spoke anything but Chinese, so conversation was out of the question; besides, it is not at all sought for by them, as they shrank away at the slightest sign of approach on our part, the reason being that they lose caste among their own people if a foreigner even chances to touch them.

After some time spent in imbibing tea and listening to the musical efforts of these syrens, we were conducted into an inner room, which was lighted by lamps hung in chains from the ceiling. Nine of us sat down to a table covered with different edibles; and as soon as one course was finished, a fresh one immediately took its place. Beside each of us was placed a damp cloth to wipe away the perspiration from our faces; and this was changed once or twice during the evening. Chop-sticks were placed for each guest; but in case we should fail to manage these satisfactorily, a sort of small pitchfork was also provided to help us out of the difficulty. But we were fully determined to gain popularity; so we manfully stuck to the chop-sticks, and with some advice as to their use, and assistance in manipulating them, we succeeded in getting on tolerably well.

This determination pleased our hosts immensely, and they were evidently flattered by our choosing the national mode of eating. I won't reveal what agony and how many abortive attempts that concession cost me!

On taking our seats—mahogany stools—the singers entered the room, and seated themselves around on ottomans behind us; to whom the custom is now and then to hand a nut or seed, or perhaps a cup of samshu, in return for which they fan you.

The post of honour is on the left of the host. The dinner commenced with birds'-nest soup, which is a white soup, and very glutinous; then came sharks' fins, which you dip first of all in various sauces on the table; then plovers' eggs; then chickens done up in different ways; claws of cray-fish, and every sort of vegetable done up in as many kinds of sauces; pastry *à l'Anglaise*, which I found very difficult to get down; other kinds of sweets, and stewed pears; the whole winding up with a dessert, consisting chiefly of crystallized fruits.

In its way, this was a more than average dinner, and our friends evidently enjoyed it immensely, taking of every dish, and that plentifully. We could not stomach it, however, and indeed took the precaution before starting of having a dinner at home to prepare us for our ordeal. I was much relieved when all the eating was over.

One of the greatest condescensions a Chinaman can make, and one of the greatest honours he can confer on you, is to take a bit from his own plate and put it into your mouth. This was done frequently, which I did not fail to return as often, much to their satisfaction.

The real task of the evening was, however, the drink. Beside each of us was placed a tea-pot containing warmed samshu, and this we drank out of small and beautifully-shaped china tea-cups. This spirit is sometimes very strong, but fortunately for us on this occasion it was rather weaker than usual. I say fortunately for us, because they seemed fully determined to see us under the table before we could satisfy their hospitable intentions; and as they were seven to two, it was very hard work for us to defeat their object, considering that the practice is anyone may challenge you to drink, when each must drain a cup of samshu, turning it up to show that you have done so. Their numbers gave them a formidable advantage, which they seemed determined to make the most of, repeatedly challenging us to drink one after the other. After some time, too, they also tried to shirk the full measure, only half filling their cups or not quite emptying them. On remarking this I immediately filled their cups for them, and made them turn them up to show they had drank it all. They were very much surprised at the liquor not having a more visible effect upon us, and indeed, so were we ourselves. At last they brought out champagne, which, although we refused at first, they made us take, saying they had procured it specially in honour of our visit. We, however, satisfied them with tasting it. While at dinner they played several games; the chief of which, as well as I could gather, was for one to hold up a certain number of fingers, and to shout out at the same time a number, when if his opponent failed to guess, without a moment's consideration, what these made together, he had to pay the forfeit of drinking a cup of samshu. They showed remarkable quickness in guessing correctly. This is quite a national custom, being generally adopted by the lower classes as an encouragement to their potations. When this lengthy repast was finished, we went out to the outer room again, and reclined on lounges, and even took a short stroll in the fresh air, which I found very soothing after our hard work.

The Chinese occupied themselves with smoking opium. We were then shown over the house. After that we had another and smaller feed; and on getting into our boat to return home, a girl presented us with a betel nut done up in a green leaf. They wanted us to stop longer, but as it was two o'clock, and we were quite done up with fatigue, we resolutely declined. They themselves probably prolonged their orgies till the morning. As the tide was running very strong with us, and as we were well manned, we went home at a tremendous pace; still, being a very dark night, we had to keep our eyes about us, to avoid collisions.

This was the only native dinner I was at, but as far as my inclinations go it was quite sufficient to last for my lifetime.

It can be seen from this description—which is of a by no means exceptional event; in fact, it is what they indulge in more or less every night in the year

—that the Chinaman is inclined to be fastidious in his eating. They linger over this meal with a fondness that shows their whole idea of happiness centres in the indulgence of good living. It is with the utmost regret that they compel themselves to leave the table, and I believe no human argument could persuade them to omit enjoying a single course. They also do not merely touch each separate dish, but they eat copiously of it. This characteristic is somewhat in contradiction to their usual abstemious and business-like habits, although I think the merchant classes, as a rule, abstain at all other times—particularly in business hours—and look upon their dinner, not only as the day's chief event, but also as the great reward of all their toil.

It cannot be said, either, that their night's orgy leaves any ill effect after it.

The next day we meet them as cool, as calculating, and as self-confident as ever; and while we who may have indulged in a heavy repast pay the penalty in a heightened pulse and a feverish frame, we see the companions and sharers of our festivities apparently as unaffected as if it had been all a dream.

These remarks do not apply to the Mandarin classes, who keep themselves entirely distinct, and quite a race apart; indeed, in many important traits they are totally dissimilar to the rest of their countrymen. But the lower we descend in the social scale out there, the greater do we find the desire for social comforts and self-indulgence, and the vice of excess in drinking is manifest to a very marked degree; at the same time, however, it is not to be seen so much publicly in the streets as it is that it exists widespread among the people, and is indulged in to a degree that altogether surpasses the outward show its victims make.

But if this vice brings its terrible evils, there is another, no less a vice, and far more deeply rooted among the masses. I refer to gambling. The middle classes are also addicted to it; but as there are social, if not legal, punishments inflicted on them, it is really in the lower classes that all the evils of this folly are to be seen. The man who can only even on great occasions risk a trifle, is a more inveterate gambler at heart than he who can lose his dollar every night without any serious inconvenience to himself. No sooner does a youth—no matter how young—obtain the smallest coin, than he immediately makes for the nearest of the gambling booths, which are very numerous throughout Canton; and although he may a hundred times before have paid the forfeit of all his earnings, he has learned no prudence from his experience, and his recklessness and trust in some good stroke of fortune that never has occurred is as great as ever; and in this respect the most confirmed *roué* who lost a fortune half a century ago at Baden or Homburg, and has ever since tried to regain it by some special and, o course, infallible system, and by limiting himself to guineas, does not surpass the poor Chinaman, who, in the utter credulity of his heart, and in his firm belief in rewards and punishments—of course shaped to his own invention and desire—on the earth, rushes to trust his all in the hands of unscrupulous sharpers, only to find that again he has thrown away his money, and that one more unsuccess has swelled the total of his failures.

This mania for speculation pervades the whole of the lower orders, and is a true and reliable proof of the real ignorance of the populace,—an ignorance which has been to a great extent hidden from us by that which, however, does not always go hand in hand with civilization, viz., a good-natured feeling of tolerance towards one another. The order of their streets, the absence of open quarrels, have imposed upon all observers; and they have considered these as signs of an intelligent understanding,—even if granting that they still cling tenaciously to the precedents of antiquity. The wonderful peace on the Canton river, which is the home of thousands of boats and junks of every size and description, is most striking. It is most unusual to hear even a verbal quarrel, while resorting to blows is a thing that never occurs.

And this is on a river where, from the strength of the current, even the utmost skill and experience cannot always avert trivial accidents. All this good behaviour has concealed the fearful ignorance that is behind it,—and, indeed, superstitions of the most degrading character are the inducements to these poor people to place an implicit reliance in the imaginary.

There is another evidence of this in the fact that they never learn to speak a foreign tongue. It is a wonderful exception to meet a Chinaman who has even a smattering of an European language. Nearly all the interpreters are Europeans. It is a rare thing to meet with a Chinese interpreter. In the upper and middle classes also the learning is limited exclusively to the sacred books, and examinations are held periodically over the country; and proficiency in the works of Confucius and of Mincius—great as the merits of these undoubtedly are—is the sole test of a liberal education. It therefore is tolerably evident that while there is no learning or knowledge of any kind among the poorer classes, even that of the upper is superficial and exceedingly limited in its extent.

A comparison with their neighbours the Japanese makes their narrow-mindedness the more apparent. Colleges are being instituted in the one for the propagation of western science and languages; and the European modes of government are being fast adopted, the management being entrusted to foreigners. Yet the other still remains like a snail coiled up in its own shell. It indeed seems a useless task to hope for any improvement from them, as the power is entirely in the hands of the Mandarins, who, as a body, are the most bitter against the admittance of strangers.

But with jealousy for Japan so strong upon them, and the incompetency of their navy to attempt to cope with that of their rival, it seems that sheer necessity will at length compel them, if only in this way, to make use of the engineering skill of England in particular, to enable them to encounter their enemy on more equal terms. This, of course, must oblige them to have more intercourse with us, and to yield us somewhat greater liberties in our communications with the country in general. At all events, the adoption of even one improvement will be a commencement, and will encourage the most foreseeing among them to agitate for a more advanced and enlightened policy; and perhaps some day they may produce a man who will set himself the Herculean task of removing some of their prejudices and of improving the general condition and knowledge of the people; when, if successful, he will as certainly earn their gratitude for having introduced an order of things that will really increase their social advantages, and, at the same time, raise them to a more eminent position in the family of nations.

CHAPTER XII.

TRIPS IN NEIGHBOURHOOD OF CANTON; FIRES, ETC.

I purpose in this chapter to give some account of short trips taken in the immediate vicinity of Canton. These will illustrate the kind of life English residents spend out there, besides in some degree showing how we stand with regard to the natives generally.

The first of these was to a place called Lee-Ming-Coon, which is about four miles up the river, where there is a large joss house. On this occasion six of us started, including two ladies, in a gig by water, while two others went in chairs by land through the city. This temple contained a great number of small rooms, which are let out to, and are much frequented by, the Chinese, who give small dinners in them.

This is hardly indicative of any very deep religious sentiment, and does not at all agree with our own feelings as to the sacredness of a place of worship. Notice has to be given a day or two before to the authorities at the temple, who then make all the preparations necessary.

While waiting for dinner we strolled about the gardens, which were certainly very beautifully laid out, and quite maintained the high reputation the Chinese have gained as ornamental horticulturists. Their general idea is extreme imitation of nature; and while everything is as regular and correct as a Dutch garden, they are not content with this effect, but introduce rockeries and variety of trees to simulate an appearance strictly in accordance with reality. The garden is divided into long avenues, either bordered by trees or low walls, while the pretty little lakes have imitation rocks and islets on them, and are completely covered with lilies. Arbours and miniature houses beautifully carved are also, somewhat too plentifully perhaps, scattered over the ground. Some of the trees were very fine, and reminded me much of our elms.

As soon as dinner was announced we returned, to find it laid out in a most cosy little room with a punkah temporarily constructed, and the table prettily decorated with flowers. We were greatly amused by seeing first one, then another face appear at the window to get a look at the foreign visitors. After a short time we had quite a crowd of the villagers of the place outside. They were very quiet, and were perfectly satisfied with the liberty of staring. After dinner we sat in an arbour singing glees and choruses, much to the amusement of our audience. But we simply astonished them when we wound up our proceedings with an impromptu Sir Roger de Coverley, and they evidently considered we had lost our senses to perform such antics on a hot day after dinner. They liked, however, to see the "foreign devils," as they respectfully term us, enjoying themselves, although I don't think it ever entered their heads to imagine that any pleasure could arise from our exertions. They probably thought it some religious or national observance, and as such respected it. Anything connected with hard work is to their minds utterly opposed to all idea of pleasure, and they are naturally so lazy, and so averse to any exertion, that even walking about is a penalty they shrink from as much as they can. They always seem glad to get home, put on a short coat, and recline on sofas, having a smoke or their hair dressed; and it was very amusing to invent some cause for an unexpected visit, when on your entrance they immediately start up quite confused, and bustle about, striving to appear as busy as possible. They invent all kinds of excuses to make you believe them, and are most anxious to discover that they have deceived you.

We did not start on our return till about ten, when instead of getting into our own boat we took passage on board a flower boat, which we had previously hired to take us back to Canton; and as it was a very clear night, the trip was pleasant. We were very merry, and as it happened to be Her Majesty's birthday, we sang all the loyal songs we could remember. The boatmen admired our loyalty, and attempted to join in the chorus. These boats are punted along by about twelve men armed with long poles. Down each side of the boat is a sort of raised deck or gangway, on which the polers stand, six on each side; so when they work well together they can give a considerable impetus to the boat. In the stern is also an immense oar worked by the women and children of the boat family, which besides guiding the boat, helps it along very much. However, this night it was slow work, as the current was running strong against us, and we did not reach home till long past twelve o'clock.

Another time we started in a yacht in the evening, also taking canoes to go up creeks, intending to dine by candle-light on some hills not a great distance off; but the wind failed us, and we were obliged to anchor, and as it was too hot to dine below, we commenced to do so on deck; but our lights attracted all the flies in the neighbourhood, so that it was with the greatest difficulty we managed to get the better of our formidable adversaries, and finish our meal.

On another occasion—a Sunday afternoon—we started to explore one of the neighbouring creeks, when we met with a slight adventure. After rowing some distance up this creek, it became too narrow for anything but paddling. On one side the banks were rather high, while on the other they were quite flat; but each side was lined with trees very similar to our poplars, while orchards seemed to extend for miles inland. Indeed, it reminded me much of some of the fruit gardens near London. Soon we came to a small stone bridge through which we could only just scrape. At the first convenient spot we landed, and wandered about while our boys made some tea. On the other side to where we were was a large temple, where some ceremony was being performed, as we heard the music and got a glimpse of a procession.

There were some Chinese about, whom we set down as overseers, or caretakers, of the fruit, but as they usually don't object to us intruding, and never before had said anything about our taking a little fruit, we unluckily began plucking that which was about. It chiefly consisted of a flat yellow fruit, resembling our gooseberry in flavour. We wandered about for some time, and were returning to our boat when we heard a man bellowing, and on looking round saw a Chinaman rushing towards us. On getting up to us he called us foreign thieves and all sorts of bad names, and went on in a towering passion, making threats. One of us luckily was sufficiently fluent in Chinese to represent to him how matters stood, but as we unfortunately had no money with us, we could not easily pacify him. Quite a crowd of Chinese had by this time collected, and if they had wished to be quarrelsome they had us completely at their mercy; but they seemed to think the whole affair great fun, and indeed the fellow appeared to be only half saved. After half an hour's palavering, we succeeded in pacifying him a little, and he was going off, but the jeers of our boatmen were once or twice too much for him, and he returned worse than ever. At last we got rid of him, and commenced our tea on the river bank, with the Chinese still around us. We soon made friends with them by giving their little ones biscuits. After this we always, when we took fruit, held it up and showed those near, and we always found that assent was given freely and by friendly nods.

During these trips I often saw even Chinese men following the national amusement of kite flying; some of which, made in imitation of birds, are so well formed as to deceive even a practised eye at some distance. The other national amusement of fireworks is much indulged in, although the chief occasion on which I saw them was on the American Festival, July 4th, when all the American houses give grand entertainments, inviting all the missionaries and some of the chief representatives of other countries. The whole festivities wind up with a display of fireworks. Some of the set pieces are good, especially those representing pagodas and peach trees in full bloom. But as a whole, their skill as pyrotechnists is inferior to our own, although sufficiently good for the practical purpose of supplying the ships trading there with rockets and other lights.

Somewhat akin to this is the subject of fires, the most horrible of all the enemies of the human race. They are of frequent occurrence at Canton, but since the partial destruction of the town in 1822 there has been no general conflagration. Owing to the great current of air blowing down the narrow streets, the slightest one would be soon fanned into alarming proportions, if there were not an efficient organization to repress its progress on the first symptoms. As soon as a fire is announced the neighbours, an effective volunteer force, band themselves under recognised leaders to oppose the common enemy, and their skill and exertions are so energetic that they are generally able to prevent it doing widespread damage. It is said some are so agile that they can run up the walls of the houses, but I cannot personally vouch for the correctness of this assertion. At all events, they must have something more than good luck to stave off a catastrophe which often seems imminent. At Macao, where I saw a considerable fire, they formed a line down to the beach, and handed buckets continually up to the scene of action. In this case their nimble mode was attended with success, but it seemed to me that if a fire once got a hold on any quarter, their organization would be utterly powerless, and as they would in all probability decline any assistance from foreigners, the result would be no less disastrous than that of 1822 was.

The only really useful instruments of repression they possess are river fire-engines, and these, of course, could only avail when it took place in the immediate vicinity of the river. Fire, therefore—not to be despised even with all the organization of our metropolitan army—is a danger to be dreaded and prepared for when at any moment we may find that it is approaching our homes with irresistible strides; and although Shameen is more favourably situated with regard to that contingency than the old factory site was, it still behoves those out there to be on their guard against a danger that has within our recollection made many homeless, and may at any moment be repeated with all its terrible suffering and loss.

CHAPTER XIII.

THE *SPARK* OUTRAGE.

I have now come in the course of my narrative to this event, which has exercised such a baneful influence on my fate, and has blasted all the hopes of success I might previously have entertained of my worldly career. The best description I can give of it is that which was honoured by appearing in the columns of the *Times* shortly after my return to England. To my at that time necessarily limited knowledge of some of the facts concerning the origin of the catastrophe, I will, however, add after this extract some of the more important details, on which also I can thoroughly rely as authentic. I must add, however, that some of these appeared in my letter in the *Times* of March 29th last :—

"CAPTURED BY PIRATES.

"Mr. Walter William Mundy, who was the only English passenger on board the *Spark*, sends us the following interesting account of the piratical outrage on the Canton river :—

"'I embarked on board the *Spark* on the 22nd of August, to proceed on business to Macao. We left Canton at half-past seven in the morning, and were due at Macao between four and five the same afternoon. The *Spark* had once been a comfortable boat enough; but the traffic had considerably outgrown its proportions, and complaints had been repeatedly made to the Company to supply a new packet. She is a paddle-wheel steamer somewhat larger than our Thames boats. To make the subsequent events the clearer, I will endeavour, to the best of my memory, to describe those parts of the ship with which my narrative has chiefly to do. The lower deck was confined exclusively to Chinese passengers, and a winding staircase near the stern led to the quarter-deck, which was for Europeans. Passing from this gangway forward, first came the saloon, then the beam of the engine, which was exposed to view; close to this, and still more forward, was the wheel-house and the captain's cabin, divided by a thin partition. A large window in the partition enabled the captain to give his instructions to the steersman with greater facility. The fore part of the deck, covered with an awning, was where the passengers generally sat. In the centre of this was another gangway for the use of the sailors, and leading from the lower deck. There were a great many native passengers, but I had the misfortune to be the only European. The crew consisted of about twenty men—Chinese and Portuguese half castes. The captain, poor Brady, was an American, and, although an utter stranger to him previous to our journey, it has seldom been my good fortune to have a nicer or more amiable companion. Shortly after leaving Canton he gave one trait of his general disposition. The purser came and told him that there was a man below who could not pay his passage, and asked what he was to do. Brady asked what sort of fellow he was. When on being told he was a coolie, with no money at all about him, he said, "Oh, let the fellow go." We had a capital run to Whampoa. After leaving here, about nine o'clock, we breakfasted. The Canton steamer to Hong-Kong and the return steamer from Hong-

Kong ought to have passed us soon after leaving Whampoa; but from some reason they were delayed, and did not pass us till after twelve o'clock, which obliged the pirates to put off their attack. The river here, where the outrage was perpetrated, is about one mile across.

"'So far, the trip had been most delightful—nothing had occurred to awaken any suspicion. I was still as wedded to the humdrum existence and safety of English life as if I were but taking a trip in the British Channel, and so little thinking of any peril, that I dozed over my cigar and book under the awning forward. I must have slept here some time, as I certainly awoke with a start; it may have been a noise, it may have been instinct of danger which roused me. Which it really was I am now unable to tell. But I immediately perceived a man rushing up the gangway towards me with a knife in his hand, and a gash across his forehead. Surprised and only half awake, my first thought was that he was a madman, and I rushed out to procure help to seize him. In attempting to do so, I was, however, met by two other men, who attacked me with knives. Quickly seeing my mistake, I rushed past them, and ran on in search of weapons, endeavouring to find out what it all meant, and to see whether any resistance was being made. I now strove to reach the passengers' gangway, to see what the Chinese were doing. In attempting this I had to run the gauntlet of several of the pirates, who wounded me in many places. Two of them here seized me, tearing my watch off, and were going to cut my fingers off for my rings, when, by a desperate effort, I managed to break loose from them. It was then that I saw the Chinese passengers sitting below, looking as unconcerned as possible. I then rushed to the stern, where I saw the poor purser holding on by his hands to the side of the ship, preparing to jump overboard, and a pirate cutting at him. Here also the chief mate was battling most courageously with one arm, while with the other he attempted to loosen a buoy. I tried to join him, but my wounds were beginning to tell on my strength, and numbers easily drove me off. With no hope left I endeavoured to retrace my steps, but was immediately attacked by two or three fresh arrivals. I here managed to get within striking distance of one, whom I succeeded in knocking down; but the success cost me dear, as his companions wounded me at the same moment desperately in the left side. How they let me retire I cannot imagine; how I was able is equally difficult for me to explain! But I was again attacked by two others armed with capstan bars, who successively knocked me down with these weapons. I rolled out of their way, and for a time was left in peace. I staggered to the wheel-house, but had to support myself on an umbrella which I picked up. I was now almost insensible, and leaned against the window I mentioned in my description of the ship. On looking down into the captain's cabin, I saw poor Brady lying stretched out on the floor, with his little dog staring mournfully into his face. This sign of fidelity consoled me even then somewhat, and, indeed, my sole wish now centred in the hope of being able to last long enough to get some chance of revenge by the arrival of assistance. After leaning here for ten or fifteen minutes, I fell on the deck from exhaustion and loss of blood. A few minutes after this the pirates, who had been plundering the ship, returned on deck, battened down the hatchways, and proceeded to count their booty close by me. They continually passed over me, stepping on and kicking me. On receiving my wound in the side, I, luckily for myself, had sufficient presence of mind to shove my handkerchief and fingers into the aperture to keep my lungs from breaking out. The pirates, either imagining I was trying to conceal something, or in brutal sport, tore my hand several times from the wound. The agony I thus endured I can never forget. How I prayed for unconsciousness! One of them motioned to me to throw myself overboard, and even pretended to do it, lifting me up in his arms. Another, whom I judged to be the chief, as he swaggered about in my hat, with a revolver and cutlass at his belt, brandishing his sword, pretended to draw it across my throat several times, to the evident delight of all his comrades. For what reason he did not carry his performance into practice I cannot possibly conceive. I was lying on the deck for six hours with these fellows close to me, but not for one instant did I lose consciousness. A junk then came alongside, when the steamer was stopped for the first time. The plunder was transferred to the junk, and they all hastened on board her, after spiking and breaking the helm.

"'Immediately on their leaving, the crew came on deck, and, rigging a helm in the stern, commenced working the ship. A Chinese merchant, procuring assistance, carried me to the saloon, placed me on a sofa, and covered me with a tablecloth to keep the cold from my wounds. All on board were so overcome that they had to be kept at their work by a copious supply of brandy. We were delayed some time in

Macao harbour before we were permitted to land, a regiment of soldiers being drawn up to receive us on the quay, and no Chinaman was allowed to leave before he was searched and his name and address were taken. When I recall the whole event, it seems like a hideous dream. It is only when I look at the proofs on my body of its horrible reality that I awake to a full sense of all my danger, and a feeling of thankfulness for my miraculous escape drives every other thought away.'"

The alleged and generally received cause of this outrage is as follows :—

The gambling tables at Macao had been losing considerably for some time, and their partners at Canton were sending a man to them with a considerable amount of dollars, said to be in a belt attached to his person. This rumour got wind in the back slums and gambling haunts of Canton, and a body of loafers and ruined reprobates, with no character to lose, and only too eager for a prey to think of any risk, combined to ease this person of his charge. Proof of this plot was obtained from one of the pirates, who was so badly wounded that he had to give himself up to the authorities, and eventually died of his injuries. He first, however, confessed, and said that he had received his wounds in a scuffle among his comrades as to the division of the spoil. He gave all the names of the party, and it was chiefly owing to his evidence that some of them were captured. He also said that an armed junk manned by forty men was to have boarded the *Spark* while they created a diversion in their favour. He stated that had there been more Europeans, or had the ship been better guarded, they would not have attempted an attack, but waited till they reached Macao, when they could have knocked their man down, and robbed him in the streets. At the commencement of the attack, when the sailors were set upon, separated one from another among the crowds of passengers, and could offer no effectual resistance, either the second engineer or the second mate, who I believe was a Portuguese, seeing that things looked hopeless, jumped overboard, and after floating for two hours was picked up by a native boat, and then transferred to a Chinaman's steam yacht which was close at hand, and must have witnessed the whole proceeding. But its owner, with national caution and want of fellow-feeling, steamed away, although these yachts are well armed, mounting several guns; doubtless deeming the course entailing least responsibility to be to inform a gun-boat—which was, I am sorry to say, commanded by an Englishman—stationed close at hand. It, however, paid no attention, although if it had got up steam at once it would have caught the whole band red-handed. The name of this boat was the *Fei-Loong*, and it was subsequently lost, with all hands, in the typhoon. This statement has been confirmed by our representatives at Canton.

All praise ought surely to be given to the endeavours of the Chinese Government for the steps their officials took to capture the culprits! China neglects to fulfil the stipulations of her treaty, she wilfully disregards her obligations as a friendly power, she inculcates into her subjects that any crime against a foreigner is laudable; yet there is no remonstrance raised, no punishment awarded.

The Mandarins and local authorities were, however, too shrewd observers of the course of public events, and knew only too well what a storm the murder of an Englishman might bring upon their heads, to neglect the appearance of deep solicitude for the result, and not to pretend earnest endeavours for the capture and punishment of the criminals. They refused all the rewards offered by the Steam Boat Company, and by the different Governments, thinking if they only got off with simply hanging a few individuals they would indeed be lucky.

The chief mate's case was a very sad one. I knew him very well, as he was for some time stationed on a ship laid up in the Canton river, the captain of which I knew, and as I spent several evenings on board her I saw him tolerably often. When I met him on the *Spark* he told me he had just been put on that line. The next and last time I saw him was when I tried to join him on deck, when he was so gallantly keeping at bay half-a-dozen assailants. The poor purser, who was also killed, left a widowed mother with many children solely relying on him. He was generally liked, owing to his quiet and agreeable character.

The captain was reported to have made a determined resistance, but it is my firm belief that he was attacked in his cabin and taken completely by surprise, as I saw him only a few minutes after the commencement stretched out on the floor of his cabin quite dead, looking so placid as to make it evident that death had been sudden and without pain. His revolver was found with several barrels missed fire, and this gave rise to the conjecture that Brady had attempted to quell a disturbance. But as this was the same the pirate chief had fired at me several times, though fortunately without its going off, it is plain how the misconception arose.

The leader of the band was a big powerful fellow, and I hear when captured fought so desperately that it cost his captors the lives of two of their best soldiers to secure him. These are all the further facts I have been able to gather, but I think they are sufficient to make the defence set up for China's non-responsibility appear in a worse light than ever. If their acts in punishment are to be considered to outbalance their neglect in repression, surely when those acts are proved to have been really deficient they are as culpable on the lesser indictment as they are on the higher one, and the only line of defence offered for their non-liability is untenable.

In my next chapter I will endeavour to give some general account of piracy.

CHAPTER XIV.

REVIEW OF PIRACY IN CHINA.

PIRACY in China may be said in some sense to owe its origin to praiseworthy intentions and honourable endeavours, and in a descent of several hundred years the motives causing it have gone through all the changes from the lofty impulse of disinterested patriotism till they have at last degenerated into mere greed for gain and love for a turbulent existence. It may be interesting to consider under what circumstances an evil, to put down which all civilized countries are now united in opinion, was not so long ago really worthy of admiration from all observers, and had the history of China at that time been of interest to the world in general, would doubtless have attracted all the sympathy that is usually bestowed upon the unfortunate.

When the Tartars had overrun the whole of China, and the Chinese, worsted in many battles, were totally unable to make any further resistance on land, there remained but two alternatives—to the timid and the weak, surrender; to the resolved and the brave, to try conclusions and tempt fortune once more on another element. The bolder ones resolved, if these conquerors could not be driven back, if to defend their beloved country was a hopeless task, that they at least would not swell their enemies' triumph by their submission, but would carry to another clime the memory of their former greatness, and found an empire under fresh auspices. They fortunately had amongst them a man who combined in his person all the varied requirements of a leader of such a band under such circumstances. He had all the knowledge and intellect to show them what to do, and all the courage and daring to be the first to execute as well as to command. Koshinga—such was the leader's name—may one day be viewed by future Chinese generations in the same light as we do King Arthur,—that mythical champion of a race which, although we have little or no claim to rank as our ancestors, is endeared to us all by the name of Britons; and should ever the subject race regain the rule of the country, we may hear more of this gallant chieftain, and his name may be the rallying word for those who may rebel against the at present dominant Tartar. He pointed out that there was no necessity to seek a more distant asylum, until it had been proved that the conqueror—whose prowess on the sea had never been put to the test—could expel them from the islands along the coast. They therefore established themselves on these islands, especially those at the mouth of the Canton river. In a few years, by intrigue and force, they ousted the Portuguese from the island of Formosa, and making it their head-quarters, the confederacy became so powerful as to defy all the efforts of their conquerors, and for a time their voice was supreme in these seas. No ship was allowed to trade without acknowledging their authority, and it became a recognised fact that for the present the Pekin Government was unable to cope with this predatory force. But when Koshinga died, the voice that had really kept down those dissensions that continually arose, threatening to destroy all the good effects of their valour and success, was hushed, and round his deathbed were sown the seeds that bore fruit in the dissolution of the band. His wife succeeded to the command, but her two chief lieutenants quarrelling, the whole settlement was divided into two camps, and there took place at sea a fearful battle, which, if a victory for the lieutenant who supported his mistress's authority, was so far a defeat as to entail ultimately the annihilation of the community. Discord among themselves thus accomplished what all the power of a great conqueror in the full tide of his triumph could not effect. The thwarted rival seceded, with the remnants of his squadron, to the established Government; and in the course of a few years, intrigue and liberal promises to the leaders, backed up by what the disintegration of the band had commenced, and what some small reverses continued, induced the whole force to accept the general amnesty offered them.

The breaking up of this force was the removal of a standing danger to the Pekin Government, and was the disappearance of the last vestige of national resistance to the Tartar conquest. Their rule over the whole country was as fully acknowledged as when our Edward ruled from Land's End to the Grampians, and from Milford Bay to the Forelands. As the Celt and Saxon had yielded to the Norman, so had the Chinese succumbed to the Tartar of the desert.

The few dissentients to this surrender departed for other seas, but communications were still kept up with their disbanded comrades on shore; and such is the superiority in physique of the boating and fishing population of the sea coast, and their love of adventure and predatory instincts are so developed as to render them only too susceptible to the gorgeous stories brought back to them by these rovers of the sea. This being so, recruiting for these piratical junks was no difficult task, and for more than a century acts of piracy occurred at frequent intervals, although no formidable established band was organized. Towards the end of the last century, however, these pirates had become bolder. No energetic measures having been taken for years to repress their actions, they had gradually become more ambitious in their aims, attracting to their standard all those who wished to throw off the trammels of the law, all the hangers-on of the gambling booths of Canton, and offering the only chance of safety to criminals either escaped from the hands of justice or those dreading falling into them, it is no wonder that this force in a short time assumed formidable proportions. They encamped on the numerous islets at the mouth of the Canton river, some of which they fortified. These afforded them all necessary shelter, a depository for their plunder, and a look-out from which to spy their prey. At first European merchantmen were unmolested, but soon even these were compelled to pay toll to these unpleasant gate-keepers. They, however, were not especially remarkable for ferocity, or for any particularly atrocious action. Two English gentlemen, who had the misfortune to fall into their power, have given a most interesting account of their customs, which they carefully studied during their enforced residence amongst them of several years. This band flourished for several years, greatly impeding commerce; but no assistance could be expected from the Pekin Government, who acknowledged their incapacity to deal with the offenders. An English squadron was at last despatched from India, and they received such a lesson at their hands as to respect the English flag for ever after. Their power being thus crippled, the whole band melted away, and the Chinese Government built forts on the islets to keep them in their possession. This was the last occasion on which they assumed such formidable proportions, but piratical outrages have been by no means unfrequent ever since, and indeed boat robberies are a daily occurrence.

In 1828 the crew of a French merchantman, *Le Navigateur*, were compelled through stress of weather to take refuge on the coast of Cochin China, where, instead of receiving the hospitable reception usually accorded to shipwrecked mariners, they received anything but kind treatment, and were forced to sell their cargo and ship. They then took passage on board of a Chinese junk bound for Macao. On the journey, the native crew, excited by cupidity—report went that these Barbarians had many dollars—formed an atrocious and bloodthirsty plan against them. On arriving safely within sight of their destination, the Chinese passengers were transferred to another junk to land. Unfortunately this hurried departure did not arouse any suspicions in the minds of the victims, and taken off their guard, separated from one another, they were all murdered by these villains. One sailor alone—after fighting courageously—although covered with wounds, succeeded in jumping overboard; and after being refused admission by several boats, was at last picked up and landed during the night at Macao. The criminals were captured in their junk, and all were executed.

I cannot discover what became of the sole survivor, who recovered from his wounds, and, I believe, died at a great age not very long ago; and although he was compensated, I believe there was no satisfaction rendered to France for the insult to her as a nation. It was done more in the light of a private present, than in atonement for suffering caused by their subjects.

For the next thirty years acts of piracy and cases of robbery occurred at frequent intervals; but no formidable band was established. Several cases of English subjects claiming compensation on account of loss suffered by them in person, or in the death of relations, were kept in an unsettled state for years, and it was only when the stern arbitrement of war had been appealed to, and the Chinese had to sue in the form of the defeated, that these claims were taken up by our Peace Commissioners, and demand for compensation was inserted as one of the provisoes of the treaty.

The treaty of Tientsin deserves some

praise at the hands of all those interested with our future in China. It is the first treaty granted to foreigners by that most conservative of governments, and, as in every other case, was only wrung from them when our soldiery were thundering at the gate of the capital, and polluting the threshold of their temples and their palaces. Every foreigner looks to this treaty and its various stipulations as the safeguard of his presence in China,—as the Magna Charta renewing and specially enunciating his right to stand and trade on Chinese territory. If all its articles were fully observed, if all the regulations were as fully carried into practice, would there be such grumbling and discontent on the part of our merchants?

After the war the general feeling of the populace was so cowed by the valour and successful superiority of Europeans, that no attempts against our merchant ships were thought of. They confined themselves to robbing their own countrymen and pillaging native packets, till at length grown bolder by impunity, they disregarded, in my case, the reputed sanctity of white men, by not only assaulting me, but also by murdering the captain and officers of the *Spark*. The fate of these officers is too much lost sight of. Their murders appeal for revenge and redress. They died manfully at their posts; and deserting the cause of these gallant and unfortunate champions of western interests is hardly a thing to be proud of.

One of the chief facilities afforded to these pirates to continue their career is, it must be remembered, supplied by their countrymen in office. Those Mandarins vested with the local authority have the power of collecting the customs; and they farm this right to the Hoppo, or tax collector, for a period of five

14

years. To support this officer in his powerful position all the gunboats stationed on the river are pressed into his service; and what with the aid only too voluntarily given by crafts of every size and description, he finds no difficulty in putting his authority into execution. These gunboats employed on such profitable service have, therefore, little time to spare in hunting up these river pests who thrive on the community at large, and are equally willing to play the part of tax gatherer one day and pirate the next. Each of these boats is armed with its letter of marque, in the shape of a much-beflowered document authorising the collection of custom dues; and although you may have paid your charge several times before, that will not save you from having to pay it to whomsoever else may demand it. This is a disgraceful state of things, and our consuls are much to be blamed for its continuance, but in a still higher degree our authorities at home.

It may be interesting to describe how this all-powerful official and despot, the Hoppo, is elected. The contract he makes with the Governor of Quang-Toung is for five years, and for that he pays between one and two million dollars. At the end of his term he is generally estimated to have seven million dollars. As a rule he cannot get his term renewed. He is then ordered up to Pekin, but at every town on the way he is taxed. When he reaches Pekin he is not admitted within the walls until he pays a heavy fee to the Imperial Treasury, and receives, moreover, a great whipping! He then is permitted to enter the city and retire into private life,—a not much richer man, if happily a wiser, than when he entered into all the perquisites and honours of the mighty post of Hoppo of the province of Quang-Toung five years before.

What can be the inducement to any man with a handsome fortune, which he must have to obtain the post, to accept a barren honour for the short space of five years, to result in such little benefit and such great personal ignominy? I often tried to discover this, but never got more than the unsatisfactory reply that the splendour of the post was the attraction in their eyes. I have often since thought that it must be the indirect means of advancing them to some post at the court of Pekin, and that their reward is calculated by the amount of treasure they bring into the Imperial coffers. This is merely my surmise, and an attempt to give a reason for one of those things that, being a national custom, there perhaps exists no known reason for.

At all events, this Hoppo is a very disagreeable fellow for us, and requires to be placed within bounds. All power, when arbitrary, runs to excess and does harm. His, with no check on his caprice, causes us much loss, our representatives much discouragement, and our country much disparagement in prestige. The Chinese have a perfect right to certain custom dues; but it is unjust to expect us to pay exorbitant rates, first of all to enrich arrogant officials, and eventually to swell the revenues of the country and the exchequers of the favourites at Pekin.

The present system of these pirates is a small number of land colleagues either in possession of a junk or in temporary alliance with one, who join for a certain occasion, and then part company; so that if not detected at once, the difficulty of proving the real culprits is considerable, as they speedily lose themselves among the mass of their fellow-citizens. Happily for the detectives, there is the one common attraction in the gambling-booths. To show the general feeling of insecurity among the officers of the river boats, several have told me that they are in continual dread of attack from some of these rascals, and never venture about without a loaded revolver—as one of them expressed it, "five barrels for the blackguards, the sixth for myself."

Therefore if at present there is no powerful confederacy to crush, there are widespread among the masses instincts which furnish all the material for confederacies similar to those once existant, and it is only a fitting opportunity that is lacking. If our large ships are not in daily dread, if the danger to individuals is not most imminent, the inconvenience and uncertainty caused by the knowledge of what is possible is rather the more increased. When the danger is before us and certain, we can prepare ourselves to meet it unflinchingly. When there is just the likelihood of being murdered in our beds, unarmed and incapable of resistance, there is all the agony of the suffering in an intensified form, and yet nothing serious may take place. The whole question is therefore one China cannot go on shirking, or we neglecting. Germany's action in her small matter with them the other day sets us a good precedent, and one we should be wise to follow in our dealings with this power. We have just signally failed in applying the high-toned morality of western justice to an important question in our Indian empire; and we have found how impossible it is to reconcile eastern chicanery and subjection with European honour and dominion. Let us profit by the lesson, which may eventually lead to bitter things, and not make the same mistake in our diplomatic intercourse with the Celestial Empire, which we are inclined to view with a far too lenient and favourable eye.

CHAPTER XV.

SUGGESTIONS AS TO SUITABLE MEASURES FOR REPRESSING ACTS OF PIRACY.

I PROPOSE in this chapter to offer some remarks on what measures should be adopted to put an end to this class of crime, of which I endeavoured in my last chapter to give some detailed account, and the necessity for repressing which none can deny. I will divide what I would suggest under the three following heads, viz.,—firstly, What share properly falls on the Chinese Government; secondly, What individual travellers and those companies which undertake their transport should do in assistance of legislation; and, thirdly, both these proving insufficient to meet the emergency, how far it is incumbent on England and other powers to interfere in the matter, either to compel action on the part of the Pekin Government, or to take the case out of their hands, in the interest of our commerce and society in general, and carry out repressive measures on their own responsibility.

To answer any or all of these queries with complete satisfaction would require an amount of legal knowledge to which I cannot lay claim; and what I venture to say on the subject I submit to the correction of those who speak with all the authority of the law. I may indeed preface by expressing my astonishment that no more powerful voice than mine has yet been raised in pointing out the pressing nature of the question. It seems to me most astonishing of all, however, that the residents out there—those most immediately concerned—should be so apathetic in the few precautions they have adopted against a recurrence of the outrage; and yet any one amongst them may at any time meet with a similar, or even sadder, fate than my own.

Firstly, as to what is incumbent on the Pekin Government; which, besides being the first and most important of all the queries, seems also at a first blush to be the only one necessary at all,—as surely it is the country's duty to see that the police is efficient, as nothing more tends to its own advantage, or to make it more respected abroad. When that police proves inefficient, special acts of legislature must be enacted, special punishments must be inflicted on the guilty, so as to show that, when the ordinary course of justice is of no avail, there are still means left on the side of the rulers that can vindicate all the outraged majesty of the law. In China more than this must be demanded at the hands of the Government. Besides these special precautions—which have by no means come into effect—there is a moral obligation to discourage all acts against the persons of strangers, which is not inculcated at all into the rising generation by their governors. Under the circumstances, we have a right to demand that some special *social* obloquy be attached to deeds of violence against us. I emphasize the word social, as punishments of that kind are the most efficacious in dealing with these people. If we do not claim our rights, things will continue getting worse and worse every day; and the remedy then will have to be so sharp and decisive, as to render it doubtful of possibility without resulting in a war.

It is a well-known fact that the theory is deeply rooted in the heart of every Chinaman, that it is not only not unjustifiable but praiseworthy even to hold no law sacred in his dealings with a "foreign devil." Can it therefore be marvelled at, if, with this first great incentive to take unfair advantage of any foreigner, added to their dislike of foreign intercourse (than which nothing is more natural, considering how it has been forced upon them), their thoughts continually run, in the towns we visit, on the subject of getting the better of us in every way imaginable? and when they proceed to violence, as their crime carries no disgrace, what deterrent effect has the punishment inflicted, when the same breath swells the virtue of the deceased for the sufferings inflicted on one regarded as hostile by themselves? The Chinese themselves, no doubt, are the more frequent victims at the hands of these river pirates, but it is equally beyond doubt that a packet *enlevement* is looked upon with glee and pleasure by a great number of the population. They may be the same criminals who but the day before upset poor Chin out of his boat for the sake of his small cargo of fish; the same motives actuated them that will to-morrow, perhaps, make them either murder one another for his share in the booty, or waylay a native merchant on his route home to his villa near the big city; but it is beyond all dispute that their attacks on such packets as the *Spark* and the *Navigateur* command the sympathy of the masses, and would meet with lenient treatment indeed if there was not the standing fear of foreign intervention. I firmly believe that to avoid that the Chinese would at one time have yielded any point. I therefore lay special stress on the importance of having some change made in the received opinion, even if it were only qualified by the public declaration that crimes against the person of foreigners are as criminal as if committed against a native. Such a declaration would not only be our most important safeguard, but would at the same time remove the real shield of the culprit. The Mandarin officials plead in extenuation that Canton is by no means in an unguarded state, and they point for proof of their assertion to the undoubtedly great number of gunboats stationed on the river. These gunboats are well manned, and in their way by no means to be despised. Their captains and some of the head officers —such as master gunners—are Europeans, mostly English. In numbers those on the Canton river ought to suffice to put down and exterminate nests of pirates. But unfortunately they are of no real use, and afford no protection beyond their immediate vicinity. They, for the most part, have fixed stations, which of course are well known, and are therefore of no avail against the present system of these freebooters, who, when they do attack a packet, take good care not to do so too near where these guardians of the peace may interfere with their actions. This system ought to be altered; strict instructions should be issued that there should be patrols at regular hours, and that other gunboats should be kept permanently cruising about. This would be throwing great difficulties in the way of evil doers, as it would be almost impossible for them to expect the good fortune of escaping with their booty, provided even they succeeded in carrying out their attack successfully.

The present easy life on this station

would doubtless be changed, as they certainly would meet with considerable resistance,—very similar probably to that incurred by our revenue officials in putting down smuggling; but that would not be at all unwelcome, as everywhere action, with its chances of speedy promotion and prize money, is preferred to a sedentary and barren charge. It would be also a matter of wise and effectual precaution, if before permitting Chinese passengers to embark they were to some extent examined, and all weapons removed from their person; and every suspicious character—one, for instance, of notoriously bad associations—should be declined a passage. A Government official might be specially delegated to this work. Perhaps, however, it may be thought this is more a question for the steamboat company to see to, than for the State to impose any restriction on their subjects journeying on one of their own rivers.

It will be seen that I consider the greatest security the Government can give is a moral one; and that the means of repression are at hand, and only require to be properly applied to have the desired effect. It is extremely doubtful, however, whether any action will be taken in the matter, unless some gentle remonstrance be addressed to the ear of the Governor of the province of Quang-Toung.

For the second question, What ought individual travellers and the Company do to increase the safety of travelling? This of course can only be agitated for, and effected by the weight of public opinion out there; and it really rests with those interested in the journeys from Canton to Hong-Kong or Macao to see that their

Company take all the necessary precautions. But it is at all events certain that the Company ought to provide guards; that arms should be freely distributed to the crew and trustworthy passengers; that the division between native and foreign passengers should be strictly maintained; and also that a sentry, with a loaded rifle, should be stationed at each gangway, with instructions to shoot the first native who attempted to break this all-important rule. It might also be advisable to erect in the centre of the vessel a bulwarked room, occupying the whole centre of the ship, including the engines and the helm, which would afford a retreat if the outer gangways were forced, whence three or four armed men could expel a whole host of such rabble as these fellows. Some of these arrangements were for a time put in force, but had long before the *Spark* affair fallen into disuetude. If the Packet Company were to make these or some such regulations, they would be performing only the duty that is incumbent on them; while, by instituting some sort of check on the character of the passengers they receive, they would be taking every reasonable precaution to render an attack from within a remote and almost impossible contingency. Against an attack from without,—that is, by *force majeure*,—there of course can be no safeguard of this kind; but no one would think of demanding it under those circumstances.

I am also informed that the legal quibble is that while the Chinese Government would be liable for a piratical attack in their realm by boarding, they are not responsible for any internal outbreak among the passengers, although the consequences may, in all likelihood, be quite as disastrous.

All individuals can do is to assist the Company to carry out the regulations framed for their protection, and, in any emergency, to place themselves at the captain's disposal and obey orders. The measures should be concerted between the Company and the Government officials. What the latter will do, and also what they expect from the Company, should be ascertained.

At present there is mutual recrimination; and the Mandarins, aware of an unfortunate feeling out there that the Company is alone to blame, and alone must be held responsible, take advantage of what I denounce as a mistaken idea to shift all the onus of the catastrophe on its shoulders, and argue with much plausibility that it was its gross neglect that gave the opportunity to a handful of ruffians to seize and plunder such a large boat as the *Spark*. It would be difficult to imagine what must have been the delight of the officials when they found they had such a good excuse ready made for them, as to be able to shift the blame on to the shoulders of somebody else ; but it does not say much for our perspicuity or love of fair play, if we permit these dastardly sycophants to escape from all the penalty by inculpating somebody else, whose greatest fault is certainly no more than for not having taken a few, doubtless necessary, precautions.

For the third question, all I will venture to say, besides suggesting it to our rulers, is that as we were one of the high contracting powers to the treaty of Tientsin, we are no less bound than the Chinese to carry out its stipulations. Why, then, while we have been quelling a slave trade in one part of the world, and destroying Malay stockades in another, have we not seen that some of our engagements were being properly attended to? If we could not spare time to attend to such a paltry affair in person, why not instruct our representatives in China to see that something was done in the matter?

There was a vague rumour going about that the present Ministry were instituting some inquiries, and if this had been persevered in, it would have been some manifestation of a perception of the importance of the subject beginning at last to dawn on the minds of our rulers. Unfortunately, this sudden fit of energy seems to have as quickly passed away, without any salutary result whatever.

People are always sceptical on the importance of anything that does not seem of pressing moment, or that does not immediately concern themselves; but a glance at the dry figures setting forth the state of our trade with China; a thought of that important beverage, tea; a mere idea of the vast size of the country, teeming with unknown wealth, and the extraordinary influence its opening may have on our own affairs and the world in general; and also that this piracy is not confined to the Canton river, but is in force on the Yang-tse, and that it is one of the most apparent and simplest means of opposition on the part of the Chinese to further intercourse,—a slight consideration of these reasons ought to be sufficient to show the all-importance of this subject, and that it is no trivial matter at all.

A step in the right direction would be that the general instructions to our consuls should be modified. At present they run in characters easily read—interfere on no account: let individuals shift for themselves.

CHAPTER XVI.

THE TYPHOON OF 1874.

The Chinese, like most barbarous or half-civilised nations, attach superstitious importance to all those phenomena of nature which thrill the hearts even of students of science with a feeling of awe; so the comet, the earthquake, even the thunder and lightning, but above all the typhoon, have a peculiar significance to their minds, as the direct manifestation of an offended deity, and the retribution of their own transgressions. There is nothing absolutely ridiculous in these sentiments; all nations in their early ages have shared them, and indeed, in their case, the pre-eminent awfulness of the typhoon would be alone a sufficient excuse for the fears of a people not too enlightened as to the causes of these outbursts of nature.

To illustrate the character of a typhoon, I will give some description of that of 1874; to find a parallel to which, in the amount of damage inflicted, and in the immense power of the hurricane, one must go back more than a generation.

Typhoon, or Tae-foong—the great wind—bears a singular resemblance to the Greek τυφων, although it can have no direct communication with it. These storms occur periodically, generally after an interval of three or four years; as that interval is exceeded, so the storms increase in intensity; and as on this occasion there had not been one for some time over the stated period, the extreme severity of that of 1874 is thus to a certain extent accounted for. One of the chief signs of the approach of a typhoon is the extraordinary fall of the barometer that takes place; but sailors experienced in these regions are also very clever at prognosticating its arrival. Another warning note is the long and heavy swell which sets in, without any apparent cause whatever. These storms do not extend, however, very much to the north of Canton, and rage chiefly between latitudes 10° and 30° N.; and although they last from twelve to twenty hours, the great violence of the storm is only three or four in duration.

This particular typhoon, which had been expected for some time previous to its occurrence by the Chinese prophets, commenced on the evening of the 22nd of September.

In Hong-Kong, where I was at the time, placards had been put up warning all the Chinese that it was approaching, and cautioning them to keep within their houses, and also to make them as secure as possible from the 18th to the 25th of September. This time their calculations—or expectations—as to its occurrence were nearly correct; but this is by no means always the case. The warning has been issued, the public have prepared to meet the emergency, the miserable have become resigned to succumb to its fury, yet the typhoon has mercifully declined to come, and everyone has his or her mind lightened of a load; only, however, on its next visit it will take ample amends for its neglect in appearing. But in the face of such a foe no precaution should be omitted, and the warning, though repeated without perhaps any need, must not yet be treated as a mere cry of "Wolf." It commenced with a wind suddenly arising about eight in the evening, which went on till three or four the following morning with great violence. From ten to two its force was at its height, when it was awful in the extreme. Every door and window was bolted and made as fast and secure as possible; typhoon bars being put up to doubly secure the windows, which, with venetians fastened firmly outside, seemed to present an impenetrable barrier to the onset. When this had been carefully seen to, there was nothing more for the inhabitants to do but to wait patiently and to prepare themselves as best they might for the ordeal. At the time, I was lying in bed recovering from my wounds, with one arm perfectly useless, and my whole system so shattered as to make me hardly able to bear this trying shock with equanimity.

As I said, the storm commenced with a violent wind suddenly springing up, and it soon became so irresistible in its might that no obstacle seemed able to retard it.

As the night wore on, the destruction increased, and each fresh blast of the hurricane was the doom of houses and of ships. The bars across the windows snapt one after the other with a report like that of cannon; and the venetians, torn from their fastenings and banging against the wall, increased the noise, till at last the wind swept them completely off, and rushed into the house with a shriek, as if about to carry everything before it. The washing stands were in the verandah, and the wind caught the jugs and basins up as if they were but leaves, and smashed them in all directions. The glass doors leading into the bedrooms were then taken bodily off their hinges, and fragments of the glass were scattered throughout the house. Many pieces fell on my bed, but I escaped without any bad cuts. The doors throughout the different corridors were the next to succumb; and now the risk became very great that the wind would lift the roof completely off the house, which actually happened to many other houses in the colony. To add to the confusion of the scene, the wind got into the pipes and put the gas out, leaving us in total darkness.

The danger from the storm is not, however, the only one to be incurred on this dreadful occasion. Robbers take advantage of the general panic and defencelessness of the inhabitants, and even proceed to incendiarism to aid them in their nefarious designs. For me personally there was to be agony piled upon agony. A bed of sickness, feverish anxiety and nervousness alone would not have enabled me to bear the trying scenes of that night with any degree of success, but as if all these were not sufficient, I had to endure being deprived of the companionship that alone seemed to give me a fictitious strength. As the hong or house I belonged to were all members of the fire brigade, on a fire being announced they had to don their uniform and go to their duty; thus leaving me alone with a Chinese boy to look after me, who, however, was quite as unnerved as myself. In fact, all the boys of the house collected in one room, and would not come out for a long time. Now and then the one who nominally had charge of me would come and ask me had I "too muchee fear."

Some of the men returned sooner than might have been expected, greatly to my relief. All their efforts had been in vain, for in the face of such an opponent man's attempts seemed ridiculous, and the fire, such as it was, had to be permitted to burn its course.

The storm was now at its height, and it

was thought absolutely necessary to move me upstairs to a room that was more safely situated and altogether stronger than my own. One by one the remainder of the men returned, wet to the skin, and hardly able to walk as their long boots were full of water. They all took refuge in this room, and brandy was in constant request to keep up my spirits, and to refresh themselves after their trying but unavailing attepts to avert a fresh danger in a possible conflagration. This room was divided from the drawing-room by folding doors, and these soon showed signs of approaching destruction. So all the assistance we could collect in the shape of coolies was called up, and with their aid drawers and boxes were piled up against them; but they were of very little use, as the wind swept them away, and they were only erected to fall again with a crash. Then they got long bamboo poles, wedging them in to support the doors, and they had to use their fireman's hatchets as hammers; but even these props were of little avail, one giving way after the other.

All this time we were burning oil lamps, which gave both a very uncertain light and also were continually meeting with accidents. Most of the men again went out; some to look after the fire, others to try and save life from the ships that were constantly being blown on shore.

How the gusts of wind howled through the house, and how I dreaded each one as it came, and with what a sigh of thankfulness I followed its departure! How I also strove to detect some lessening in its violence, and with what heart-sinking I seemed to think each blast but louder and more terrific than its predecessor!

The poor boys wandered about, keeping

clear of the windows and our temporary barricades, lest they should come down; but every now and then my particular friend would repeat his former inquiry, and I think it was a great consolation to him to see a white man almost as frightened as himself. At last this night of horrors drew towards a close, and about four in the morning it became perceptibly quieter, and had so far softened down that at six o'clock I was able to get some sleep.

Although by no means long in duration, the oldest inhabitant at Hong-Kong could not remember one more severe. Besides the reason I gave to account for its extraordinary violence, I may mention the following, viz., that its extent was more limited, and we got it from every quarter in the course of the twelve hours. Generally its force is divided by its violence being expended in attacks at different points, separated from each other by hundreds of miles. In this instance all its might was spent on that part of the coast bordering on the Canton river, of which Hong-Kong and Macao are the seaports. Of course it was very bad over a much more extended surface, but it was here that it reached its acme. Most men who before had often expressed a wish to witness a typhoon, changed their minds after this experience of the reality, and their only desire now was never again to be subjected to its miseries and horrors.

For a week afterwards there was a complete stoppage of all work, and the various events of the catastrophe, and each individual's experience, were the sole topics of the hour.

What a sad and wretched sight Hong-Kong presented the next day! In our own house—one of the best built, and therefore one of the most fortunate in the place—the *débris* of furniture, of pictures, and of glassware cumbered the floors; smashed doors, cracked walls, and frameless apertures, that once were windows gay with venetians, on all sides! Everything in confusion, everything more or less ruined, as if the whole place had just been sacked by a victorious foe after a heavy bombardment. And the work of restoration to anything like order, beset with difficulties in every way. No carpenters or skilled workmen to be obtained at any price, so that for two or three days the house lay open to robbers, who took every advantage of the general defencelessness, until at last we had boards nailed across as a temporary protection. Hardly a single house escaped without almost the total loss of its tiles. A report was circulated that someone had purchased all the tiles in the town immediately previous to the typhoon, and that he made a fortune by selling his eagerly sought for stock at a large profit.

The Praya, or public walk along the quay, was the public meeting-place and general resort of crowds coming to see the ruins of what once had been the fine quay. This was literally torn up from its foundations, although constructed of immense blocks of granite. It looked as if "the treasure of nature's germins had tumbled all together, even till destruction sickened," and walking on the uneven surface was no easy or pleasant task. Many of the contiguous houses had been breached by some huge block being hurled against them, as if from a catapult. Some of these blocks were so imbedded in the walls as to seem to form part of the original structure. Nearly all the piers were destroyed; one of them was cut completely in two by a large steamer, which had left its anchors. Two other steamers, the *Albay* and the *Leonor*, which had just arrived with a large number of Chinese passengers, came into collision, and sank one on the top of the other. By this latter accident alone, over 150 persons were supposed to have been drowned; and during the next day, and for several days after, the odour along the quay from dead bodies and certain kinds of merchandise, carried on shore by the tide, was extremely offensive.

The *Alaska*, a Pacific mail steamer, was beached high and dry on the opposite shore; most of the coasting and other steamers had to loose their anchors and steam about. The admiral's ship and also the police hulk drifted from their moorings, and were found in totally different positions when it had all subsided. All sailing vessels were more or less injured, and for days after gunboats cruised about to bring in water-logged or otherwise disabled vessels, of which there were a great many, not a few being too much damaged to be of any further service.

It must be remembered that the roadstead of Hong-Kong is considered one of the safest and most commodious along the whole coast. Of course the greatest loss of life occurred amongst the Chinese population, especially among those living in boats. These, stationed round the colony, were all swamped. It was therefore next to impossible to discover the number of persons killed; but I believe the bodies of over 500 persons were recovered.

The prison at Kow-Loon, or Stonecutter's Island, had the roof carried off; and the Town Hall, besides suffering much general damage, had a rather fine clock spoilt. The Library also suffered a great deal. The beauty of Hong-Kong was deprived of one of its chief ornaments by the destruction of the trees lining the road to Happy Valley. These were either torn up by the roots and blocked the road, or were so damaged that they had to be cut away, as only the stumps, peeled of their bark, remained. It was some days before the road was fit again for traffic. The Governor's house, at the Peak, was unroofed, and the flagstaff which signals all incoming steamers was rendered useless. The telegraph wires also to Saigon were broken, so that messages had to be taken by steamer to Singapore or Shanghai, as the up-coast wire to Shanghai was also broken.

At Pook-foo-Lun, where the English residents have built summer bungalows, these houses, chiefly constructed of matting, were in great danger. One was blown bodily—furniture and all—into the sea. Its occupants only escaped with their lives by rushing out in their sleeping clothes, and seeking shelter behind the remaining wall of the wash-house, where they passed the remainder of that fearful night, in perfect misery and wretchedness.

Cargo boats used for trans-shipping goods were in great demand, and could only be procured by paying a heavy premium. All the racing and regatta boats, of which there were a great many, and of which the colony was very proud, were destroyed by the hulk of a vessel being blown through the roof of the boat-house. The swimming baths were also ruined. Most of the private steam-launches had either capsized or been swamped. One of the Canton Steamboat Company's steamers had a large hole knocked in her side; and there were many other incidents to show the general destruction, which would, however, be tedious to relate.

It can, therefore, easily be imagined how wretched and sad the harbour looked, with wrecked hulks floating about, or the masts of ships projecting above the surface of the water.

I understand, however, that Macao suffered to a greater extent even than Hong-Kong. The bodies of over 4,000 Chinese were recovered, not a boat was left uninjured in the place, gunboats were either overturned. or landed high and dry, and one steamer was *reported to have been blown three miles inland.*

The Canton steamer to Macao, *White Cloud*, was fouled by a junk, sunk, and was of no use afterwards.

Fires were also more numerous here than at Hong-Kong, and some assumed alarming proportions. These were set down as the acts of incendiaries, and there were many daring robberies. The soldiers were called out to put down these disorders, but refused to obey, and the Macaese had to be armed in self-defence, as a last resource to restore order in the state of anarchy and turmoil that was rampant in the island for several days. The destruction was so extensive, that when I left China it was considered extremely doubtful whether such a poor place could ever recover. The only prospect was that the Chinese might think it worth their while to rebuild it themselves.

So ended the great typhoon of 1874, which, for its violence and for the damage inflicted by it, may compare with any of the greatest catastrophes that have become historical. It must be remembered that, besides the direct loss, there was much injury done to the country by the wind blowing the salt inland for miles, which cast a blight on all vegetation. It cannot be accurately estimated how much damage was inflicted, but it certainly cannot have been less than several millions sterling in this neighbourhood alone.

While the natives seemed during its duration completely crushed with terror, afterwards, when they were able to review their altered circumstances, their natural apathy returned to enable them to bear the accumulated losses they found they had incurred. But although, with care and hard work, a few years will doubtless remove all traces of the destruction of property, it will require a much longer time before the black images of that terrible night shall be equally blotted out from their memory. Those who, like myself, saw it for the first, and also probably for the last time, must ever retain a most vivid remembrance of its terrific grandeur; although I, personally, had no loss in any way to lament by it; and indeed my altered circumstances and departure for home afforded me too many subjects to occupy my attention, to permit me to indulge in any unnecessary recurrence to a painful and unpleasant event.

CHAPTER XVII.

CONCLUSION.

But a few days elapsed after the occurrence of the typhoon, when it was decided by my medical attendants that a return to Europe was absolutely necessary for me, as longer residence in China had become an impossibility, through the shattered state of my nervous system. I will only look on that fact as the cause for the end of my narrative. I will make no remark here on the far more important bearing that decision had on my own destiny. In the course of this narrative I have endeavoured—with what success my readers must determine—to show the mode of life followed by English residents in China; while I have at the same time attempted the more ambitious task of considering those topics that seem most pressing in their character, occasioned by our intercourse with the Chinese. I am perfectly aware of the responsibility I have incurred by commenting as freely as I have on political subjects that may by some be considered beyond the province of such an unpretending book as mine. I may seem to have neglected the real object of my story for the sake of saying something about matters of a more fascinating character than the dry details of daily life in Canton. But my answer to such objections is, that my whole idea in writing this relation of my brief residence was to familiarise —even to such a small degree as I am able —the public to some knowledge of Chinese matters. In doing so, where topics of general interest have seemed naturally suggested, I have ventured to comment upon them; and in this I think I have not exceeded my right. I have also devoted three chapters to piracy, and have done my best to view that public evil in as impartial a light as possible.

Residence in China may be taken to be a state of existence that requires much luxury and amusement to make it endurable; but as those necessaries are always obtainable, there is no discontent on the part of the English residents. The insecurity always experienced, and the uncertainty of approaching events, have, however, greatly increased since my departure; and indeed, if it is generally imagined out there that they are living on the sides of a volcano that may any day explode to their destruction, occurrences of too recent date to need specific mention have been such as to give some ground for their worst fears. For it must be clearly understood that there is no friendly communication whatever between the natives and ourselves. We never ask them to our houses, we never go to theirs; we are never seen in general conversation with any of them; when we do dine together, it is at the Flower Boats, in a hired room; we are not, even on these rare occasions, admitted to any very great degree of intimacy, although our entertainers are of course of the more convivial or youthful description. The restraint is increased by our ignorance of one another's tongue. An English resident for years will only know a few words, or at the most a smattering of business verbiage. The Chinaman is still less proficient. But it is certainly for us to learn out there; and a spirit of emulation ought to possess all Englishmen to attain to a certain fluency in the native language as rapidly as possible. Perhaps such knowledge, besides being of immense practical use, might be also of some political weight, and might tend to lessen the prejudices at present existing on both sides.

I have also ventured to speak strongly in favour of the speedy introduction of the steam engine, and believe that the fact of Whampoa being to all purposes the port of Canton, presents a very suitable occasion to inaugurate such an experiment, and one at the same time presenting no inordinate difficulties, both because the natives are there most familiar to the presence of the foreigner, and also on account of the shortness of the journey.

But I will no longer linger over what I have previously narrated. My subject is one of daily increasing importance. China is rapidly occupying as much of attention as India; and papers which before treated Chinese questions as beneath their notice, are now continually instructing the public by articles on their customs, their military or naval progress, and the movements of Christian missionaries; and even the disagreements with ourselves are turned to profitable account by increasing our acquaintance with this strange nation. There therefore can be no question as to the importance of my theme; but when I consider the manner in which I have been able to treat it, it is then that I feel my own unfitness to do so in an adequate way. Many of my readers, I dare say, have spent as many years in China as I have months; some, perhaps, much longer; others who have never been there have made her history a life-long study. What will these say as to the propriety of my writing, when they, with all their acquaintance, or with all their knowledge, have remained silent? I may be permitted to say that they are the only proper persons to furnish the reply. But from the general reader who has followed me through my reminiscence of a happy six months in a far distant land, I feel assured that I shall receive nothing but consideration. That re-awakening of past events has not been accomplished without some pain, and to recall how swift was the passage from a pleasant existence to a bed of sickness and a blank career has been no pleasant operation. I will end as I commenced, by expressing that the highest reward I could possibly expect to result from what I have written would be to set an example that might be followed with more brilliant success by those more versed in Chinese life than myself. If in any way or on any single point my remarks have made something more comprehensible, or have put questions in a clearer light, my book has served its purpose, and I am content. To elucidate the hidden mysteries of any national character; to point in any way, be it never so slight, to a mode of making peoples better affected one towards the other; to view the actions of those we are brought in contact with so as to enable us to appreciate their virtues and condone their faults,—each one of these objects is sufficient to honour the attempt of anyone, were he even such an humble instrument of use as myself.

SEPTEMBER, 1875.

SAMUEL TINSLEY'S

PUBLICATIONS.

London:

SAMUEL TINSLEY,
10, SOUTHAMPTON STREET, STRAND.

⁎ *Totally distinct from any other firm of Publishers.*

NOTICE.

The PRINTING *and* PUBLICATION *of all Classes of* BOOKS, *Pamphlets, &c.—Apply to* MR. SAMUEL TINSLEY, *Publisher,* 10, *Southampton Street, Strand, London,* W.C.

SAMUEL TINSLEY'S
NEW PUBLICATIONS.

THE POPULAR NEW NOVELS, AT ALL LIBRARIES IN TOWN AND COUNTRY.

A DESPERATE CHARACTER: a Tale of the Gold Fever. By W. THOMSON-GREGG. 3 vols., 31s. 6d.

"A novel which cannot fail to interest."—*Daily News.*

ALDEN OF ALDENHOLME. By GEORGE SMITH. 3 vols., 31s. 6d.

"Pure and graceful. . . . . Above the average."—*Athenæum.*

ALICE GODOLPHIN and A LITTLE HEIRESS. By MARY NEVILLE. In 2 vols. 21s.

A NAME'S WORTH. By Mrs. M. ALLEN. 2 vols., 21s.

ANNALS of the TWENTY-NINTH CENTURY; or, the Autobiography of the Tenth President of the World-Republic. 3 vols., 31s. 6d.

"From beginning to end the book is one long catalogue of wonders. . . . Very amusing, and will doubtless create some little sensation."—*Scotsman*

"By mere force of originality will more than hold its own among th rank and file of fiction."—*Examiner.*

"Here is a work in certain respects one of the most singular in modern literature, which surpasses all of its class in bold and luxuriant imagination, in vivid descriptive power, in startling—not to say extravagant suggestions —in lofty and delicate moral sympathies. It is difficult to read it with a serious countenance: yet it is impossible not to read it with curious interest, and sometimes with profound admiration. The author's imagination hath run mad, but often there is more in his philosophy than the world may dream of. . . . We have read his work with almost equal feelings of pleasure, wonderment, and amusement, and this, we think, will be the feelings of most of its readers. On the whole, it is a book of remarkable novelty and unquestionable genius."—*Nonconformist.*

AS THE FATES WOULD HAVE IT. By G. BERESFORD FITZGERALD. Crown 8vo., 10s. 6d.

Samuel Tinsley, 10, Southampton Street, Strand.

A WOMAN TO BE WON. An Anglo-Indian Sketch. By ATHENE BRAMA. 2 vols., 21s.

"She is a woman, therefore may be wooed ;
She is a woman, therefore may be won."
—TITUS ANDRONICUS, Act ii., Sc. 1.

"A welcome addition to the literature connected with the most picturesque of our dependencies."—*Athenæum.*

"As a tale of adventure "A Woman to be Won" is entitled to decided commendation."—*Graphic.*

"A more familiar sketch of station life in India . . . . has never been written. . . . ."—*Nonconformist.*

". . . . Very well told."—*Public Opinion.*

BARBARA'S WARNING. By the Author of "Recommended to Mercy." 3 vols., 31s. 6d.

BETWEEN TWO LOVES. By ROBERT J. GRIFFITHS, LL.D. 3 vols., 31s. 6d.

BLUEBELL. By Mrs. G. C. HUDDLESTON. 3 vols., 31s. 6d.

"Sparkling, well-written, spirited, and may be read with certainty of amusement."—*Sunday Times.*

"Contains a number of spirited sketches of places and people . . . will while away an idle hour very pleasantly."—*Daily News.*

BORN TO BE A LADY. By KATHERINE HENDERSON. Crown 8vo., 7s. 6d.

"Miss Henderson has written a really interesting story. . . . The 'local colouring' is excellent, and the subordinate characters, Jeanie's father especially, capital studies."—*Athenæum.*

BUILDING UPON SAND. By ELIZABETH J. LYSAGHT. Crown 8vo., 10s. 6d.

"It is an eminently lady-like story, and pleasantly told. . . . . We can safely recommend 'Building upon Sand.'"—*Graphic.*

CHASTE AS ICE, PURE AS SNOW. By Mrs. M. C. DESPARD. 3 vols., 31s. 6d. Second Edition.

"A novel of something more than ordinary promise."—*Graphic.*

CINDERELLA: a New Version of an Old Story. Crown 8vo, 7s. 6d.

CLAUDE HAMBRO. By JOHN C. WESTWOOD. 3 vols., 31s. 6d.

CRUEL CONSTANCY. By KATHARINE KING, Author of 'The Queen of the Regiment.' 3 vols., 31s. 6d.

"It is a very readable novel, and contains much pleasant writing."—*Pall Mall Gazette.*

Samuel Tinsley, 10, Southampton Street, Strand.

DISINTERRED. From the Boke of a Monk of Carden Abbey. By T. ESMONDE. Crown 8vo., 7s. 6d.

DR. MIDDLETON'S DAUGHTER. By the Author of "A Desperate Character." 3 vols., 31s. 6d.

DULCIE. By LOIS LUDLOW. 3 vols., 31s. 6d.

FAIR, BUT NOT FALSE. By EVELYN CAMPBELL. 3 vols., 31s. 6d.

FAIR, BUT NOT WISE. By Mrs. FORREST-GRANT. 2 vols., 21s.

FIRST AND LAST. By F. VERNON-WHITE. 2 vols., 21s.

FLORENCE; or, Loyal Quand Même. By FRANCES ARMSTRONG. Crown 8vo., 5s., cloth. Post free.

"A very charming love story, eminently pure and lady-like in tone, effective and interesting in plot, and, rarest praise of all, written in excellent English."—*Civil Service Review.*

FAIR IN THE FEARLESS OLD FASHION. By CHARLES FARMLET. 2 vols., 21s.

FOLLATON PRIORY. 2 vols., 21s.

FRIEDEMANN BACH; or, The Fortunes of an Idealist. Adapted from the German of A. E. BRACHVOGEL. By the Rev. J. WALKER, B.C.L. Dedicated, with permission, to H.R.H. the PRINCESS CHRISTIAN of SCHLESWIG-HOLSTEIN. 1 vol., crown 8vo, 7s. 6d.

GAUNT ABBEY. By ELIZABETH J. LYSAGHT, Author of "Building upon Sand," "Nearer and Dearer," etc. 3 vols., 31s. 6d.

GOLD DUST. A Story. 3 vols., 31s. 6d.

GOLDEN MEMORIES. By EFFIE LEIGH. 2 vols., 21s.

"There is not a dull page in the book."—*Morning Post.*

GRAYWORTH: a Story of Country Life. By CAREY HAZELWOOD. 3 vols., 31s. 6d.

Samuel Tinsley, 10, Southampton Street, Strand.

GRANTHAM SECRETS. By Phœbe M. Feilden 3 vols. 31s. 6d.

"The plot is comparatively new, and, though rather complicated, is well worked out; and some of the characters are delineated with considerable force and appreciation of dramatic effect. . . . . The story is gracefully written, and has a tone of wholesome earnestness and purity throughout."—*Scotsman.*

"It is undoubtedly what many people would call a very pleasing story. . . . . . The merit of this book consists in its refined tone, and in the real touches of nature which greet us in the character of Margaret. The story shows considerable promise, and some power over the passions."—*Pall Mall Gazette.*

GREED'S LABOUR LOST. By the Author of "Recommended to Mercy," etc. 3 vols., 31s. 6d.

HER GOOD NAME. By J. Fortrey Bouverie. 3 vols., 31s. 6d.

"Abundance of stirring incident . . . and plenty of pathos and fun justify it in taking a place among the foremost novels of the day."—*Morning Post.*

HER IDOL. By Maxwell Hood. 3 vols., 31s. 6d.

HILDA AND I. By Mrs. Winchcombe Hartley. 2 vols., 21s.

"An interesting, well-written, and natural story."—*Public Opinion.*

"For a novel of good tone, lively plot, and singular absence of vulgarity, we can honestly commend 'Hilda and I.'"—*English Churchman.*

HILLESDEN ON THE MOORS. By Rosa Mackenzie Kettle, Author of "The Mistress of Langdale Hall." 2 vols., 21s.

"Thoroughly enjoyable, full of pleasant thoughts gracefully expressed, and eminently pure in tone."—*Public Opinion.*

HIS LITTLE COUSIN. By Emma Maria Pearson, Author of "One Love in a Life." 3 vols., 31s. 6d.

IN BONDS, BUT FETTERLESS: a Tale of Old Ulster. By Richard Cuningham. 2 vols., 21s.

IN SECRET PLACES. By Robert J. Griffiths, LL.D. 3 vols., 31s. 6d.

IS IT FOR EVER? By Kate Mainwaring. 3 vols., 31s. 6d.

Samuel Tinsley, 10, Southampton Street, Strand.

JOHN FENN'S WIFE. By Maria Lewis. Crown 8vo., 7s. 6d.

KATE BYRNE. By S. Howard Taylor. 2 vols., 21s.

KATE RANDALL'S BARGAIN. By Mrs. Eiloart, Author of "The Curate's Discipline," "Some of Our Girls," "Meg," &c. 3 vols., 31s. 6d.

KITTY'S RIVAL. By Sydney Mostyn, Author of 'The Surgeon's Secret,' etc. 3 vols., 31s. 6d.

"Essentially dramatic and absorbing. . . . . We have nothing but unqualified praise for 'Kitty's Rival.'"—*Public Opinion.*

LADY LOUISE. By Kathleen Isabella Clarges. 3 vols., 31s. 6d.

LALAGE. By Augusta Chambers. Crown 8vo, 7s. 6d.

LEAVES FROM AN OLD PORTFOLIO. By Eliza Mary Barron. Crown 8vo, 7s. 6d.

LORD CASTLETON'S WARD. By Mrs. B. R. Green. 3 vols., 31s. 6d.

"Mrs. Green has written a novel which will hold the reader entranced from the first page to the last."—*Morning Post.*

MARGARET MORTIMER'S SECOND HUSBAND. By Mrs. Hills. 1 vol., 7s. 6d.

MARRIED FOR MONEY. 1 vol., 10s. 6d.

MARY GRAINGER: A Story. By George Leigh. 2 vols., 21s.

MR. VAUGHAN'S HEIR. By Frank Lee Benedict, Author of "Miss Dorothy's Charge," etc. 3 vols., 31s. 6d.

MUSICAL TALES, PHANTASMS, AND SKETCHES. From the German of Elise Polko. Crown 8vo, 7s. 6d.

NEARER AND DEARER. By Elizabeth J. Lysaght, Author of "Building upon Sand." 3 vols., 31s. 6d.

Samuel Tinsley, 10, Southampton Street, Strand.

NEGLECTED; a Story of Nursery Education Forty Years Ago. By Miss JULIA LUARD. Crown 8vo., 5s. cloth.

NO FATHERLAND. By MADAME VON OPPEN. 2 vols., 21s.

NORTONDALE CASTLE. 1 vol., 7s. 6d.

NOT TO BE BROKEN. By W. A. CHANDLER. Crown 8vo., 10s. 6d.

ONE FOR ANOTHER. By EMMA C. WAIT. Crown 8vo, 7s. 6d.

ONLY SEA AND SKY. By ELIZABETH HINDLEY. 2 vols., 21s.

OVER THE FURZE. By ROSA M. KETTLE, Author of the "Mistress of Langdale Hall," etc. 3 vols., 31s. 6d.

PERCY LOCKHART. By F. W. BAXTER. 2 vols., 21s.

PUTTYPUT'S PROTÉGÉE; or, Road, Rail, and River. A Story in Three Books. By HENRY GEORGE CHURCHILL. Crown 8vo., (uniform with "The Mistress of Langdale Hall"), with 14 illustrations by WALLIS MACKAY. Post free, 4s. Second edition.

"It is a lengthened and diversified farce, full of screaming fun and comic delineation—a reflection of Dickens, Mrs. Malaprop, and Mr. Boucicault, and dealing with various descriptions of social life. We have read and laughed, pooh-poohed, and read again, ashamed of our interest, but our interest has been too strong for our shame. Readers may do worse than surrender themselves to its melo-dramatic enjoyment. From title-page to colophon, only Dominie Sampson's epithet can describe it- it is 'prodigious.'"—*British Quarterly Review.*

RAVENSDALE. By ROBERT THYNNE, Author of "Tom Delany." 3 vols., 31s. 6d.

"A well-told, natural, and wholesome story."—*Standard.*
"No one can deny merit to the writer."—*Saturday Review.*

RUPERT REDMOND: A Tale of England, Ireland, and America. By WALTER SIMS SOUTHWELL. 3 vols., 31s. 6d.

Samuel Tinsley, 10, Southampton Street, Strand.

Samuel Tinsley's Publications.

SAINT SIMON'S NIECE. By FRANK LEE BENEDICT, Author of "Miss Dorothy's Charge." 3 vols., 31s. 6d.

From the **Spectator**, July 24th:—"A new and powerful novelist has arisen . . . We rejoice to recognise a new novelist of real genius, who knows and depicts powerfully some of the most striking and overmastering passions of the human heart . . . It is seldom that we rise from the perusal of a story with the sense of excitement which Mr. Benedict has produced."

From the **Scotsman**, June 11th:—"Mr. Frank Lee Benedict may not be generally recognised as such, but he is one of the cleverest living novelists of the school of which Miss Braddon was the founder and remains the chief. He is fond of a 'strong' plot, and besprinkles his stories abundantly with startling incidents . . . The story is written with remarkable ability, and its interest is thoroughly well sustained."

SELF-UNITED. By Mrs. HICKES BRYANT. 3 vols., 31s. 6d.

Westminster Review:—"'Self-United' has many marks of no ordinary kind . . . The style is excellent, the conversation bright and natural, the plot good, and the interest well sustained up to the last moment."

SHINGLEBOROUGH SOCIETY. 3 vols., 31s. 6d.

SIR MARMADUKE LORTON. By the Hon. A. S. G. CANNING. 3 vols., 31s. 6d.

SKYWARD AND EARTHWARD: a Tale. By ARTHUR PENRICE. 1 vol., crown 8vo, 7s. 6d.

SPOILT LIVES. By MRS. RAPER. Crown 8vo, 7s. 6d.

SOME OF OUR GIRLS. By Mrs. EILOART, Author of "The Curate's Discipline," "The Love that Lived," "Meg," etc., etc. 3 vols., 31s. 6d.

"A book that should be read. . . . Ably written books directed to this purpose deserve to meet with the success which Mrs. Eiloart's work will obtain."—*Athenæum*.

"Altogether the book is well worth perusing."—*John Bull*.

SONS OF DIVES. 2 vols., 21s.

STANLEY MEREDITH: a Tale. Crown 8vo, 7s. 6d.

STRANDED, BUT NOT LOST. By DOROTHY BROMYARD. 3 vols., 31s. 6d.

SWEET IDOLATRY. By MISS ANSTRUTHER. Crown 8vo, 7s. 6d.

Samuel Tinsley, 10, Southampton Street, Strand.

THE ADVENTURES OF MICK CALLIGHIN, M.P., a Story of Home Rule; and THE DE BURGHOS, a Romance. By W. R. ANCKETILL. In one Volume, with Illustrations. Crown 8vo, 7s. 6d.

THE BARONET'S CROSS. By MARY MEEKE, Author of "Marion's Path through Shadow to Sunshine." 2 vols., 21s.

THE BRITISH SUBALTERN. By an Ex-SUBALTERN. 1 vol., 7s. 6d.

THE D'EYNCOURTS OF FAIRLEIGH. By THOMAS ROWLAND SKEMP. 3 vols., 31s. 6d.

THE HEIR OF REDDESMONT. 3 vols., 31s. 6d.

THE INSIDIOUS THIEF: a Tale for Humble Folks. By One of Themselves. Crown 8vo., 5s. Second Edition.

THE LOVE THAT LIVED. By Mrs. EILOART, Author of "The Curate's Discipline," "Just a Woman," "Woman's Wrong," &c. 3 vols., 31s. 6d.

"Three volumes which most people will prefer not to leave till they have read the last page of the third volume."—*Pall Mall Gazette.*

"One of the most thoroughly wholesome novels we have read for some time."—*Scotsman.*

THE MAGIC OF LOVE. By Mrs. FORREST-GRANT, Author of "Fair, but not Wise." 3 vols., 31s. 6d.

"A very amusing novel."—*Scotsman.*

THE MISTRESS OF LANGDALE HALL: a Romance of the West Riding. By ROSA MACKENZIE KETTLE. Complete in one handsome volume, with Frontispiece and Vignette by PERCIVAL SKELTON. 4s., post free.

"The story is interesting and very pleasantly written, and for the sake of both author and publisher we cordially wish it the reception it deserves." —*Saturday Review.*

THE SECRET OF TWO HOUSES. By FANNY FISHER. 2 vols., 21s.

THE SEDGEBOROUGH WORLD. By A. FAREBROTHER. 2 vols., 21s.

THE SHADOW OF ERKSDALE. By BOURTON MARSHALL. 3 vols, 31s. 6d.

Samuel Tinsley, 10, Southampton Street, Strand.

THE SURGEON'S SECRET. By Sydney Mostyn, Author of "Kitty's Rival," etc. Crown 8vo., 10s. 6d.

"A most exciting novel—the best on our list. It may be fairly recommended as a very extraordinary book."—*John Bull.*

THE THORNTONS OF THORNBURY. By Mrs. Henry Lowther Chermside. 3 vols., 31s. 6d.

THE TRUE STORY OF HUGH NOBLE'S FLIGHT. By the Authoress of "What Her Face Said." 10s. 6d.

"A pleasant story, with touches of exquisite pathos, well told by one who is master of an excellent and sprightly style."—*Standard.*

THE WIDOW UNMASKED; or, the Firebrand in the Family. By Flora F. Wylde. 3 vols., 31s. 6d.

TIMOTHY CRIPPLE; or, "Life's a Feast." By Thomas Auriol Robinson. 2 vols., 21s.

"This is a most amusing book, and the author deserves great credit for the novelty of his design, and the quaint humour with which it is worked out."—*Public Opinion.*

TIM'S CHARGE. By Amy Campbell. 1 vol., crown 8vo, 7s. 6d.

TOO LIGHTLY BROKEN. 3 vols., 31s. 6d.

"A very pleasing story . . . . . very prettily told."- *Morning Post.*

TOM DELANY. By Robert Thynne, Author of "Ravensdale." 3 vols., 31s. 6d.

"A very bright, healthy, simply-told story."—*Standard.*

"All the individuals whom the reader meets at the gold-fields are well-drawn, amongst whom not the least interesting is 'Terrible Mac.'"—*Hour*

"There is not a dull page in the book."—*Scotsman.*

TOWER HALLOWDEANE. 2 vols., 21s.

TOXIE: a Tale. 3 vols., 31s. 6d.

TWIXT CUP and LIP. By Mary Lovett-Cameron. 3 vols., 31s. 6d.

"Displays signs of more than ordinary promise. . . . As a whole the novel cannot fail to please. Its plot is one that will arrest attention; and its characters, one and all, are full of life and have that nameless charm which at once attracts and retains the sympathy of the reader."—*Daily News.*

Samuel Tinsley, 10, Southampton Street, Strand.

Samuel Tinsley's Publications.

TWIXT WIFE AND FATHERLAND. 2 vols., 21s.

"A bright, vigorous, and healthy story, and decidedly above the average of books of this class. Being in two volumes it commands the reader's unbroken attention to the very end."—*Standard.*

"It is by someone who has caught her (Baroness Tautphoeus') gift of telling a charming story in the boldest manner, and of forcing us to take an interest in her characters, which writers, far better from a literary point of view, can never approach."—*Athenæum.*

TWO STRIDES OF DESTINY. By S. BROOKES BUCKLEE. 3 vols., 31s. 6d.

UNDER PRESSURE. By T. E. PEMBERTON. 2 vols., 21s.

WAGES: a Story in Three Books. 3 vols., 31s. 6d.

WANDERING FIRES. By Mrs. M. C. DESPARD, Author of "Chaste as Ice," &c. 3 vols., 31s. 6d.

WEBS OF LOVE. (I. A Lawyer's Device. II. Sancta Simplicitas.) By G. E. H. 1 vol., Crown 8vo., 10s. 6d.

WEIMAR'S TRUST. By Mrs. EDWARD CHRISTIAN. 3 vols., 31s. 6d.

"A novel which deserves to be read, and which, once begun, will not be readily laid aside till the end."—*Scotsman.*

WILL SHE BEAR IT? A Tale of the Weald. 3 vols., 31s. 6d.

"This is a clever story, easily and naturally told, and the reader's interest sustained throughout. . . . A pleasant, readable book, such as we can heartily recommend."—*Spectator.*

WOMAN'S AMBITION. By M. L. LYONS. 1 vol., 7s. 6d.

THIRTIETH THOUSAND.

YE VAMPYRES! A Legend of the National Betting Ring, showing what became of it. By the SPECTRE. In striking Illustrated Cover, price 2s., post free.

Samuel Tinsley, 10, Southampton Street, Strand.

ROBA D'ITALIA; or, Italian Lights and Shadows: a record of Travel. By CHARLES W. HECKETHORN. In 2 vols., 8vo, price 30s.

THE EMPEROR AND THE GALILEAN: an Historical Drama. Translated from the Norwegian of HENRIK IBSEN, by CATHERINE RAY. In 1 vol., crown 8vo, 7s. 6d.

ETYMONIA. In 1 vol., crown 8vo, 7s. 6d.

HOW I SPENT MY TWO YEARS' LEAVE; or, My Impressions of the Mother Country, the Continent of Europe, the United States of America, and Canada. By an Indian Officer. In one vol. 8vo. Handsomely bound. Price 12s.

FACT AGAINST FICTION. The Habits and Treatment of Animals Practically Considered. Hydrophobia and Distemper. With some remarks on Darwin. By the HON. GRANTLEY F. BERKELEY. 2 vols., 8vo., 30s.

MALTA SIXTY YEARS AGO. With a Concise History of the Order of St. John of Jerusalem, the Crusades, and Knights Templars. By Col. CLAUDIUS SHAW. Handsomely bound in cloth, 10s. 6d., gilt edges, 12s.

ON THE MISMANAGEMENT OF THE PUBLIC RECORD OFFICE. By J. PYM YEATMAN, Barrister-at-Law. In Wrapper, price 1s.

LETTER TO THE QUEEN ON HER RETIREMENT FROM PUBLIC LIFE. By One of Her Majesty's most Loyal Subjects. In wrapper, price 1s., post free.

THE USE AND ABUSE OF IRRATIONAL ANIMALS; with some Remarks on the Essential Moral Difference between Genuine "Sport" and the Horrors of Vivisection. In wrapper, price 1s.

CONFESSIONS OF A WEST-END USURER. In Illustrated Cover, price 1s.

THE STOCK EXCHANGE UNMASKED. In Wrapper, price 1s.

Samuel Tinsley, 10, Southampton Street, Strand.

Samuel Tinsley's Publications.

HARRY'S BIG BOOTS: a Fairy Tale, for "Smalle Folke." By S. E. GAY. With 8 Full-page Illustrations and a Vignette by the author, drawn on wood by PERCIVAL SKELTON. Crown 8vo., handsomely bound in cloth, price 5s.

"Some capital fun will be found in 'Harry's Big Boots.' . . . The illustrations are excellent, and so is the story."—*Pall Mall Gazette.*

MOVING EARS. By the Ven. Archdeacon WEAKHEAD, Rector of Newtown, Kent. 1 vol., crown 8vo., 5s.

A TRUE FLEMISH STORY. By the Author of "The Eve of St. Nicholas." In wrapper, 1s.

THE PHYSIOLOGY OF THE SECTS. Crown 8vo., price 5s.

ANOTHER WORLD; or, Fragments from the Star City of Montalluyah. By HERMES. Third Edition, revised, with additions. Post 8vo., price 12s.

THE FALL OF MAN: An Answer to Mr. Darwin's "Descent of Man;" being a Complete Refutation, by common-sense arguments, of the Theory of Natural Selection. 1s., sewed.

THE RITUALIST'S PROGRESS; or, A Sketch of the Reforms and Ministrations of the Rev. Septimius Alban, Member of the E.C.U., Vicar of S. Alicia, Sloperton. By A. B. WILDERED, Parishioner. Fcp. 8vo. 2s. 6d. cloth.

MISTRESSES AND MAIDS. By HUBERT CURTIS, Author of "Helen," etc. Price 1d.

EPITAPHIANA; or, the Curiosities of Churchyard Literature: being a Miscellaneous Collection of Epitaphs, with an INTRODUCTION. By W. FAIRLEY. Crown 8vo., cloth, price 5s. Post free.

"Entertaining."—*Pall Mall Gazette.*
"A capital collection."—*Court Circular.*
"A very readable volume."—*Daily Review.*
"A most interesting book."—*Leeds Mercury.*
"Interesting and amusing." *Nonconformist.*
"Particularly entertaining."—*Public Opinion.*
"A curious and entertaining volume."—*Oxford Chronicle.*
"A very interesting collection."—*Civil Service Gazette.*

TWELVE NATIONAL BALLADS (First Series). Dedicated to Liberals of all classes. By PHILHELOT, of Cambridge; in ornamental cover, price sixpence, post free.

Samuel Tinsley, 10, Southampton Street, Strand.

POETRY, ETC.

THE DEATH OF ÆGEUS, and other Poems. By W. H. A. Emra. Fcp. 8vo., 5s.

HELEN, and other Poems. By Hubert Curtis. Fcp. 8vo., 3s. 6d.

MISPLACED LOVE. A Tale of Love, Sin, Sorrow, and Remorse. 1 vol., crown 8vo., 5s.

THE SOUL SPEAKS, and other Poems. By Francis H. Hemery. In wrapper, 1s.

SUMMER SHADE AND WINTER SUNSHINE: Poems. By Rosa Mackenzie Kettle, Author of "The Mistress of Langdale Hall." New Edition. 2s. 6d., cloth.

THE WITCH of NEMI, and other Poems. By Edward Brennan. Crown 8vo., 10s. 6d.

MARY DESMOND, AND OTHER POEMS. By Nicholas J. Gannon. Fcp. 8vo., 4s., cloth. Second Edition.

THE GOLDEN PATH: a Poem. By Isabella Stuart. 6d., sewed.

THE REDBREAST OF CANTERBURY CATHEDRAL: Lines from the Latin of Peter du Moulin, sometime a Prebendary of Canterbury. Translated by the Rev. F. B. Wells, M.A., Rector of Woodchurch. Handsomely bound, price 1s.

THE TICHBORNE AND ORTON AUTOGRAPHS; comprising Autograph Letters of Roger Tichborne, Arthur Orton (to Mary Ann Loder), and the Defendant (early letters to Lady Tichborne, &c.), in facsimile. In wrapper, price 6d.

BALAK AND BALAAM IN EUROPEAN COSTUME. By the Rev. James Kean, M.A., Assistant to the Incumbent of Markinch, Fife. 6d., sewed.

ANOTHER ROW AT DAME EUROPA'S SCHOOL. Showing how John's Cook made an Irish Stew, and what came of it. 6d., sewed.

Samuel Tinsley, 10, Southampton Street, Strand.

Samuel Tinsley's Publications.

NOTICE.—SECOND EDITION.

UNTRODDEN SPAIN, and her Black Country. Being Sketches of the Life and Character of the Spaniard of the Interior. By HUGH JAMES ROSE, M.A., of Oriel College, Oxford; Chaplain to the English, French, and German Mining Companies of Linaries; and formerly Acting Chaplain to Her Majesty's Forces at Dover Garrison. In 2 vols., 8vo., price 30s.

The Times says—"These volumes form a very pleasing commentary on a land and a people to which Englishmen will always turn with sympathetic interest."

The Saturday Review says—"His title of 'Untrodden Spain' is no misnomer. He leads us into scenes and among classes of Spaniards where few English writers have preceded him. . . . We can only recommend our readers to get it and search for themselves. Those who are most intimately acquainted with Spain will best appreciate its varied excellences."

The Spectator says—"The author's kindliness is as conspicuous as his closeness of observation and fairness of judgment; his sympathy with the people inspires his pen as happily as does his artistic appreciation of the country; and both have combined in the production of a work of striking novelty and sterling value."

The Athenæum says—"We regret that we cannot make further extracts, for 'Untrodden Spain' is by far the best book upon Spanish peasant life that we have ever met with."

The Literary Churchman says—"Seldom has a book of travel come before us which has so taken our fancy in reading, and left behind it, when the reading was over, so distinct an impression."

OVER THE BORDERS OF CHRISTENDOM AND ESLAMIAH; or, Travels in the Summer of 1875 through Hungary, Schlavonia, Bosnia, Herzegovina, Dalmatia, and Montenegro to the North of Albania. By JAMES CREAGH, Author of "A Scamper to Sebastopol." 2 vols., post 8vo, 25s.

ITALY REVISITED. By A. GALLENGA (of *The Times*), Author of "Country Life in Piedmont," &c., &c. 2 vols., 8vo., price 30s.

CANTON AND THE BOGUE: the Narrative of an Eventful Six Months in China. By WALTER WILLIAM MUNDY. Crown 8vo, 7s. 6d.

LONDON IN THE WORKS OF CHARLES DICKENS. By T. EDGAR PEMBERTON, Author of "Under Pressure." Crown 8vo, 6s.

www.ingramcontent.com/pod-product-compliance
Lightning Source LLC
Chambersburg PA
CBHW032114230426
43672CB00009B/1733